MW01656797

THE JOY OF SERVANT MOTHERHOOD

One Mom's Journey

MARIE MOZZI

Copyright © 2023 by Marie Mozzi

Cover Art: Jan Saunders

Cover Design: Larry Smith

Additional Illustrations: Reed Scott Adler

Interior Formatting: Maria Connor

No part of this book may be reproduced in any form or by any electronic or mechanical means, including information storage and retrieval systems, without written permission from the author, except for the use of brief quotations in a book review.

Ebook ISBN: 979-8-9882764-0-1

Print ISBN: 979-8-9882764-1-8

Contents

Praise for The Joy of Servant Motherhood

In *The Joy Of Servant Motherhood,* you truly will feel the "joy"! All motherhood is service...but grasping the joy in the day to day of motherhood is something I often forget and have forgotten to do. In this lovely book, part memoir and part instructional, I was reminded about the true joys of a life in service to my own two daughters, and was given an opportunity to reflect on my journey with my children. May you read Marie's book and discover the joy within the service of that blessed title, "mom"!

-Sarah Hart, Award-winning Musician, Songwriter, Speaker

I found so much to relate to in *The Joy of Servant Motherhood.* So many memories came flooding back to me! This book is filled with tons of practical wisdom and advice for mothers. Pretty sure fathers will gain a lot of insight as well! A great reminder that when we learn to serve, we truly live well.

-Gus Lloyd, Seize the Day, Sirius XM-The Catholic Channel

To my sweet daughter Kate... You are a gift, my angel.

God graced me with being your mom, and I am so grateful. You have forever changed me.

Acknowledgments

It takes a village to write a book, and I never thought I'd embark on this journey. It has been all that and more—a magnificent, eye-opening journey filled with humility, love, tears, and growth.

Throughout my life, I've always been grateful for the hundreds of people I've met: teachers, mentors, and influencers. I was open to listening and embracing the relationships I cultivated and the lessons and gifts they shared. As I wrote this book, I realized that I wouldn't have been the mom I was without all these incredible people and communities that embraced my love, my life, and Kate. It would take volumes to thank all the people who challenged me to deepen my faith, and who helped me keep learning as I carried out my work as a mom.

To my wonderful husband, Chuck. This book would never have happened without your love and support. You believed in my dreams and my abilities to be an author. Our meeting, our life, and our love is no accident, and God brought us together for a reason. I am forever grateful for you and for us.

To Karen, Bob, and Don, my siblings who have and will always be my true tribe. The inspiration and memories we shared served me well as I wrote this book. I love you.

Mom, I love you for who you are and what you taught me. I pray for your peace, comfort, and happiness.

To Dad, I miss you. You appeared in a dream to me just a year ago and said, "I will make it right by you." I didn't know what that meant. Perhaps writing this book has something to do with the message? I'm not sure, but it's done. Your love continues to be here on earth.

Anthony, my silent, stoic son-in-law. Thank you for loving Kate and for the man you are. I am so happy to call you son-in-law.

Thanks to my "book tribe." This overwhelming project became a reality with your guidance and help. To Reno Lovison, for your creativity, ideas, and endless rewrites and discovery sessions you lead me on to help me peel the onion and let go of the committee working overtime in my head. Your talent and efforts are so appreciated. Virginia McCullough, my editor, and ever-present motherly guide, what a gift you have been on this project. You pushed me to dig deeper into my writing. It made this book even more meaningful because of your nudging. Maria Connor, thanks for your magic in putting this book together. To get it right, Jan Saunders, thank you for your beautiful artwork on the cover and your patience in listening to the Holy Spirit as I was. It's perfect. Thank you, Larry Smith, for taking this artwork and making it come alive.

To Sister Evelyn Craig, my spiritual friend, guide, and mentor. Late-night conversations with you at John Carroll University had a purpose thirty-five years ago. All these years, you have walked the spiritual path with me, affirming my love for our Lord and the desire to serve and live my faith. Your guidance helped me to listen to and meet Jesus by embracing His voice, seeing Him in all things, and staying present even when the darkness came in. Thank you for encouraging me to jump into the shadows and trust God. I'm happy to still walk with you on this faith journey.

To *everyone* who has ever coached, taught, and shared knowledge and inspiration with me. I heard and embraced what you said.

To my daily mass extended family, Ann C, Joe and Eileen, Maryanne, Pat, Ann, JeanEmily, and Cathy, Maria and Paul, your faith inspires me. What would I do without our early morning coffee sessions, get-togethers, and the encouragement, laughter, and tears we've shared? You have helped me come to know Jesus in new and beautiful ways. There is a deep meaning behind the coffee, cookies, and conversations we share. You will always be in my prayers.

Foreword

Was I surprised the woman who claimed she hated to write had decided to write a book? Yes, for sure. Was I surprised this was the topic? Not in the least. Was I a little teeny-tiny bit nervous that she was about to put all of my dirty little secrets on blast for the world to read? Yes, again. Yet, despite a lifelong frustration with writing, she took the time to write a book about being a mom. Nothing shocked me about that.

My mother has been a busy woman her entire life. Her many different careers include, but aren't limited to spa director, aerobics instructor, consultant, and director of the church youth group. She's earned multiple educational degrees/certificates—a bachelor's degree in Theology, a certification in spiritual direction and leadership training. Mom also has mastered many hobbies. For one thing, she loves to bake, especially her incredible, and secret recipe, oatmeal chocolate chip cookies. She's now an avid and skilled tennis player. I used to be able to beat her, but that ship has sailed. Parishioners attending daily mass enjoy the gift of her beautiful voice. She's a great dancer, and I can't forget her ballroom competitions—just like "Dancing with the Stars." The list is truly endless.

I'm one of the lucky ones. No matter what else was going on in Mom's life, I knew with certainty she'd always be there for me. Whether it was staking out a spot in the front row of one of my volleyball games or sitting on my bed while we played with each of my stuffed animals, she was there. Physically, emotionally, and mentally present.

Even from a young age, I saw Mom take pride in being a mother. She wanted to be a good mother of a child who knew she was loved every second of every day. I've been blessed to have a close relationship with her all my life, and for many years it was just the two of us. We spent those years dancing, traveling, baking, learning, playing, experiencing. So many laughs, and occasional tears, but always fun and lots of love. When she told me she intended to share some experiences and stories about being my mom, it actually made a lot of sense. I am who I am because of her. The stories she's choosing to share in this book have shaped me into a strong, independent, and only mildly stubborn woman. I'll be forever grateful to my mother for the life she's given me and the experiences we've shared.

I enjoyed reliving some of the heartfelt experiences and moments Mom describes in the book. I hope you, too, appreciate her stories and take away ideas that can help you on your motherhood journey. (Oh, one last thing. The story about the salad in Chapter 13...believe me, I've *never* spoken to my mother that way. Maybe I'll tell you *my* version of the story someday.) My mother's love and respect for moms everywhere, regardless of their circumstances, comes through on every page.

Congrats, Mom. I'm really proud of you. I love you.

Kate Boi
May 2023

ONE

What Is Servant Motherhood, Anyway?

The fastest way to break the cycle of perfectionism and become a fearless mother is to give up the idea of doing it perfectly—indeed to embrace uncertainty and imperfection.

—Arianna Huffington

Motherhood brings with it a wide range of intense emotions. One day we're filled with joy, and the next day we're begging for reinforcements. We do everything we can to eventually send the best children possible into the world. The desire to do our best lingers in the wings every day, but sometimes it feels like one step forward and three steps back. But what keeps us going is the joy of raising our children to be the best they can be, and the way to do that is to lead from the heart, which is the foundation of being a servant mom.

What does it mean to be a servant leader and to lead from the heart? Fundamentally it's about finding the strengths in others and helping them soar. It's about finding value in others and putting their best interests first.

This is where it gets tricky. The word servant conjures up the image of someone whose role or job is to wait on other people or take of everything for another person or group of people. But when it comes to servant leadership, specifically servant motherhood, putting others first most definitely doesn't mean putting yourself last. It means understanding you are in a leadership position, and it's your duty to look out for the best interests of your team, in this context, your family.

Servant leaders, or servant moms, accomplish this by making their team members better and by encouraging them to be their best, but not by supplying all of the answers and constantly telling them what to do. Like servant leaders in all settings, as servant moms we demonstrate our ability to put ego aside and then step back and let the individuals we lead exercise their own strength and independence under our guidance. We serve by being guides. We serve by being leaders.

So often the word "leader" itself carries connotations of power, an inflated ego, and the notion of "my way or the highway." But that's not true of servant leaders. In the business world, successful servant leaders motivate and empower others to be their best because they know their group or team is only as good as their people. Likewise, in the world of servant mothers —or parents—the family is the group or team. Family leaders understand the adage that the whole is greater than the sum of the parts. Strong capable individuals should equal a strong capable group. Servant leaders in all arenas lead by example, doing the things they would ask their team, or family, to do.

And what does this have to do with motherhood? Everything! In accepting my role as a mom, I'd put aside my agenda in order to serve my daughter lovingly and willingly. It meant her needs were the priority. Early on my journey, I was well aware that serving my daughter meant I was to set the example by walking the talk. Her observations of my actions and the sincerity around my attitude of "serving" would create her foundation for being a future leader herself.

My intention, my resolve, was put to the test many times. For example, I was challenged to avoid complaining about my to-do list and hectic schedule. No griping about how tired I was from working all day and then driving an hour away to a volleyball game, only to come home to household chores and overseeing homework. It was about getting up on winter mornings in Northern Michigan to shovel feet of snow so I could walk the dog, get Kate to school, and then head off for a full day of work. Even though I might relish a quiet night to myself, I needed to rearrange my plans when my child wanted to talk. When we serve others, their needs often pop up at the most inconvenient times, but the effects of showing up can be life-changing for you and for those you lead.

Listening, encouraging, and empowering are examples of what we do as moms—servant mothers. It all matters. We help our kids do the right thing and we strive for a loving, peaceful family life, and also manage the unexpected hiccups along the way. Ultimately, your family benefits and society benefits:

Strong capable, caring individuals = Strong capable, caring families = Strong capable, caring communities.

BUMPS IN THE ROAD

In no way am I implying that the job of a servant mom is an easy one, or without potholes and snares that threaten the quest. In my early days as a young mother, I struggled. I'd married my best friend and was a Navy wife. As an officer on a naval submarine, my husband was away from home for extended periods. To be clear, he was—and is—a good man and we got along fine, but as it turned out, we didn't share mutual agape love. I was troubled by the state of our marriage, but at the same time my heart hurt from what I later discovered were issues of my own and a lot of baggage I carried with me from childhood.

I continued to struggle with my own painful difficulties even after Kate was born. By that time, I also realized that regardless of what happened with my marriage, I was committed to leaving my personal baggage behind. At all costs, I'd avoid dragging my "stuff" into my quest to raise a healthy, loving child.

When my husband left the military, he accepted a new job in a different state and we prepared to move, which is when a host of issues came to a head for me. I had deep connections in the community we were leaving behind, including my friends and others who were my "family of choice." I also had a fulfilling job as a youth minister in our parish. My husband left to start his new job, but I stayed behind for six months while our house sold. Quietly, privately, I was okay with this because I already feared where our marriage was heading.

I was in deep emotional turmoil over what felt like a devastating move. I was scared and distraught and also coped with my guilt over things that weren't working out according to plan. I lived in this fear and deep sadness for weeks before we moved. At that time, I'd had a number of losses in my life and this move was now the icing on the cake. In fact, I was physically sick the days the packers came, and then, when the movers arrived to load the truck, I had to leave the house. My life, my safe place that housed so many early memories with Kate was being taken away box by box. When the house was empty, I went back in by myself, and the tears began to flow. I felt empty, lost, and in some way abandoned.

That abandonment piece continued to resurface in my life. Not surprisingly, I later found out that abandonment issues were a root challenge for me and showed up often in my journey from childhood to adulthood. This is why I was acutely aware that I didn't want my child ever to feel insecure or alone. While I was raising my daughter, I never intended to share this part of my story and recount these struggles. I'm doing so now, because I now realize that I wasn't alone in trying to come to terms with internal troubles and issues that if left unaddressed would likely have interfered with becoming the best servant mother—and leader—I could be.

At the time, though, I was petrified to leave behind a life in which I was connected and go forward to a place where I couldn't ignore the fact that my marriage was dry and troubled. To top it off, I had guilt and a heavy heart over my Catholic belief that marriage was supposed to be for a lifetime. Living with that was incredibly painful, along with the pressure of feeling that I was a failure at marriage, but not yet knowing what to do. Despite this, I worked hard to keep pain and distress away from my servant motherhood role.

Kate was two years old when we moved to Ohio. My determination to make a better life for her was my saving grace and the strongest motivation to heal and change. The morning after I arrived at our new home and Kate's dad had left for work, I tried to muster some enthusiasm for the task at hand and dove into the tedious chore of unpacking boxes. Soon my heart began to race, then tears welled up. Before long I fell into a heap, sobbing among the chaotic fragments of my life strewn around me. I cried tears like never before. The heartache was overwhelming.

In this painful state, I thought about my friend, Diane, who I also considered my spiritual mom. I'd begun to confide in Diane shortly after Kate was born and she had an uncanny ability to read—or hear—between the lines. From a Christian perspective and an empathetic heart, Diane listened to me talk about my issues stemming from childhood and my current fears about my marriage. Diane had suggested that once the move took place I should seek professional counseling. Given the depth of my distress and sadness at the start of this new life, I was certain it was time to dig into what had been causing me such pain. It was critical that I unravel any patterns that could interfere with my important role as a mother.

I started by contacting my husband's employee assistance program, which resulted in a rather disastrous first intake visit (described later). After that rocky start, though, I persisted and was given an appointment with June Ruse, PhD, a psychotherapist, who also happened to be a lawyer. Something about the "aura" in Dr. Ruse's office told me I was in the right place. I soon was reassured that Dr. Ruse was sincere in wanting to help me on this phase of my journey. I was able to share my story, answer questions, and feel supported. I was ready to embrace the journey of addressing deeper issues.

As my first session concluded, Dr. Ruse gave me some homework. I was to buy three books we'd be using in our sessions: *Codependent No More* (Melody Beattie), *Toxic Parents* (Susan Forward) and *The Dance with Intimacy* (Harriet Lerner). I left the appointment with a glimmer of hope—my first in a long time. That same day I bought the three books at a bookstore and began to read them that very day. All three are modern classics about healing and growth, and you can find them in most any library. (See the Resource list for more information about these and other books.)

Page by page, chapter by chapter I read every word in each book by the time of my next appointment. What I'd read led to numerous revelations and deep introspective work, some of which shook me a little and disturbed my sense of who I was and what I carried with me from childhood. Still, I eagerly embraced all that was revealed. In this short time, I already felt much different than I had at the start of the process. I'd also opened Pandora's Box. However, as new insights emerged, my anxiety lessened, curiosity took over, and I found comfort in anticipating what might be revealed next. With the therapist's help, I continued to dig deep, discovering and unraveling a tapestry of emotions—love, abandonment, avoidance issues, and so much more. I had a strong desire to be a successful woman in my own right and to confidently embrace my newest role of servant mom.

FINDING WHAT WE NEED TO HEAL

After only a few appointments with Dr. Ruse I was on my way. Over the next few months, I worked through a discernment process that led me to initiate a separation from my husband. We subsequently divorced and our marriage was annulled. Kate and I moved 90 miles away, closer to my family than I'd been in years. In our new town, I researched therapists and scheduled an appointment with a new counselor, Faith. Nothing ironic about her name. My personal faith was and continues to be the foundation of my life and my character, especially during what turned out to be a two-year journey towards self-actualization and healing.

Along with therapy, my Catholic faith was and is the rock that creates the place from which I move every day. Faith understood that I wanted to be a successful mother, but that my own strength and wellbeing had to come first in order to authentically ground myself in my role as Mom. We continued to work through emotional wounds, and I began to heal patterns in my life that had led to both anxiety and avoidance.

She helped me unravel and discard many negative scripts that had been misguiding my head and heart. I embarked on more self-help reading and additional modalities that positively influenced my life for years to come. Faith was a special woman and a gifted therapist. When I saw her for the last time before relocating again, I brought Kate to the visit. At one point Faith gestured to her and said, "You know now about loving unconditionally, right?"

"I believe so," I answered.

"You do. And do you know how I know that?" Faith pointed to Kate. "Right there. You love that little girl completely, unconditionally. You know it, and she knows it as well. Now get in the boat and row, and just keep on rowing."

I'll never forget Faith's words. From the onset of this internal work, I focused on getting this mom thing right. No rules, courses, or instructions would help if I didn't confront my own issues first.

Being a mom felt natural, as is the case for many women, but at the same time I feared venturing down the road of a dysfunctional mother-daughter relationship. My deepest desire was to raise my daughter from a healthy, confident place. And because of the help I sought and received, that's what I did. Ultimately, it's why I wrote this book.

LETTING GO OF THE PAST

Even without knowing a single detail of your story, I assume that you want nothing more than to be the best servant mom you can be. In order to fulfill that for myself, it meant admitting that I needed help. I had to heal myself so I could be the mother I wanted to be for Kate. Many of us look good on the outside, meaning that we seem to have it all together. I had what looked like a "successful childhood," if that's measured by grades and activities, and even accolades and prizes. My servant's heart was always looking to improve the situation or lives of others. Those around me assumed I had it together.

Later, I realized how different my external life was from what had been going on inside. When I married, I thought I knew what love was but obviously that wasn't the case. Then I struggled in a marriage even though I'd been confident in my belief I could be successful in that kind of partnership. That wasn't true, either. The strength I obtained in learning about myself in counseling and other efforts was priceless.

I've always been successful at endeavors I put my mind to. I'm also an empath, which means I operate from a place of service, often putting others first. As a mother, it's important that we put the needs of our children at the forefront, and that's also the mindset of a servant leader, or as I saw myself, a servant mom. The needs of others, in this case my daughter, were crucial in order to get the best from her and for her. It wasn't about spoiling Kate or trying to be her friend. It was about being authentic and acting from a place of grace and confidence. And it was also learning how to take care of myself by making room for me at the top of the list. Self-care and my own inner work would help me stay true to myself and to my family.

I became aware that avoiding my own baggage from the past was a recipe for failure as a servant mom, and that realization is behind the motivation to pass on to you what I've learned. As a servant mom it was important that I be a good example. I quickly learned that if I didn't address "my stuff," Kate couldn't come first. My baggage would unconsciously resurface in my actions, discipline, and mothering traits. Not the kind of servant mom I aspired to be.

The point is, that we're all dysfunctional in some way or carry some uncomfortable experiential baggage. But we can each strive to make it better for ourselves and for the sake of our children. Making sense of my own life has had a trickle-down effect. If I take care of understanding my emotions, my child will stand a better chance of making sense of her emotions as she faces her own life challenges.

As a single mom for most of Kate's life, I wasn't out to be a supermom, but simply one who chose to live from a healthy, loving place. Sure I made mistakes and would have appreciated a few do-overs here and there. What I do know is that in any endeavor, I lead from a much stronger place after asking for help. I learned to turn to God and remain humble and open to unpack uncomfortable issues, and dive in and admit that I'm vulnerable and without answers. Over time, answers and confidence were and are revealed. My heart-centered work as a mom meant that I'd lead from that place—from my heart. I know that is where God lives, so I listen. From there I work, I try, I fall, but I get up again and just keep going.

YOU ARE NOT ALONE

As a servant mom, I learned to take initiative. In other words, I encountered circumstances in which there were no concrete directions and no time to wait for protocols on mothering. Sometimes a need is in front of us and we need to jump in and *get 'er done*. At the same time, I'm humbled and aware that I'd have been unsuccessful if I'd chosen to make this journey alone. God provided the strength I needed to take on my servant motherhood role one day at a time. If not for my faith and the gift of His grace, I'd have been in a different place entirely on this journey of motherhood. I'm certain of it. I'd have managed to make it through, but without the added grace to be a mother with confidence and compassion coming from a heart-centered place.

It's in the spirit of servant leadership that I approached this book. I've laid out the reasons I sought help, and also urge you to look within yourself to identify areas where you might need healing or guidance. I also have experience in the pitfalls of finding the right professional counselor. The whole process of finding appropriate help can be difficult, even remarkably painful, especially because we're usually vulnerable in the first place, or certainly not coming from our most confident place.

As I said earlier, my search for help started by going through my husband's employee assistance program, which had its particular protocols in place, all of which were new to me. Still, it took only a week before I had an appointment with an intake or evaluation counselor, who'd I see for three sessions, at which point the next steps would be determined. I was nervous and a bit skittish about what to expect but I embraced the opportunity with an open heart and open mind. I wanted to deal with this emotional pain and disappointment and was willing to face other issues that would inevitably come up.

Driving into downtown Toledo, Ohio, for the first appointment also was new territory for me, but I was determined. The vintage brick office building looked tired, but I confidently headed up to the office in the elevator. At the designated floor, I stepped into an enormous, empty waiting room and took a seat in this uninspiring space. Minutes later, a man entered the room. As he approached, my heart raced and my palms began to sweat. No disrespect to scientists, but the guy reminded me of a worn-out and stereotypical "mad scientist" with wiry hair and dark-rimmed glasses. Holding a lit cigarette in his hand, he walked towards me and asked, "Are you Marie?"

Managing a timid but affirmative response, I followed him. That was it. Not knowing exactly what to expect, it seemed an awkward introduction. I trailed somewhat cautiously behind him, certain I was walking towards a dungeon. As I entered his clinic, my fear of a dungeon was spot on. To say I was appalled and shocked at the sight is an understatement. It seemed like a bad dream. Dark, dingy, and dirty, the office overflowed with stacks of books, magazines, and endless paperwork. The couch had barely enough space for me to sit. Dirty ashtrays were everywhere. I've always hated cigarette smoke. What a nightmare.

Dr. X sat across from me and asked why I was there. After feebly stumbling through my story and explaining my feelings, challenges, and emotional hiccups, Dr. X asked a few questions. Nothing felt natural about this. At the end of the session, he looked at me and said, "Well, here's what I think. Number one, you're not in love with your husband. Number two, stop feeling sorry for yourself, and number three, get out and get involved."

I was speechless. He wasn't wrong about point number one. But moving on to his second statement, I was certain there was much more to my situation than simply feeling sorry for myself. As to his third point, it turned out that one of my challenges was getting *over* involved, likely as a way to avoid what was really going on in my life. Back then I already led from a servant's heart and for me saying no was the challenge. Even an enthusiasm for God can lead to over-commitment.

This whole scene played out like a very bad movie. I left the building in a state of shock. Maybe I hadn't known what to expect, but I was pretty sure this was not how it was supposed to go. At home, my husband asked how it went. Standing in the stairway between our first and second floor I leaned against the wall crying, and then slid to the floor in a heap. "What a disaster!" At this point I was beyond confused and feeling worse than I had the day or week before. Now what?

Sadly, this is the kind of experience that causes too many people to give up. They might say to themselves, "Who needs this humiliation? I already feel awful." Some people may have heard negative things about counselors and "shrinks" and now those impressions have been confirmed. Or, some people may have others, including family members and close friends, telling them not to trust psychologists or any type of therapist.

These misadventures into the world of counseling are not uncommon and can be enormously hurtful and counterproductive. But that's not the time or reason to give up. Quite the opposite. Instead of pulling back, dig in and search elsewhere. Consult trusted friends, faith leaders, doctors, and others. Community mental health centers often offer a variety of good counseling choices on a sliding fee scale. If you seek help, you deserve to receive competent, trained counselors who will listen and offer help.

When I called Diane the next day and recounted my experience, she was appalled and affirmed my sense that nothing about this was the way a first appointment with a counselor was supposed to unfold. With her encouragement, I called the employee assistance program and conveyed my story in detail. The intake person offered an apology and assured me someone would get back to me right away.

In this new and unfamiliar environment, my path toward help could have been derailed by a bad counselor, but because I was persistent, I was given another appointment, this one with Dr. June Ruse, the first of two counselors who was able to guide my path to healing. I urge you to do the same and persist. You'd go to any length to find the right help for your children, and you can do the same for yourself.

YOU ALWAYS HAVE SUPPORT

Living as a faith-inspired servant mom meant I had support. I certainly had spiritual support when seeking help for myself. Comfort and direction were always available in times of adversity. I learned about creating space to just *be*. God accepted me where I was, and knowing that, I wanted to be better, do better, and feel comfortable in my being. This meant taking time to be alone with my own thoughts and to do some healing so I wouldn't be a victim of my past. It meant being still and listening to God, not easy for an active mom. But in wanting to do the best for Kate and to lead by example, I learned to surrender and give up control.

I began to embrace servant motherhood qualities and chose a life with my daughter that would ultimately develop servant leadership qualities in her. I truly believe that through this experience God was slowly nurturing the traits I needed in order to be an effective servant leader and servant mom. By serving out of love and charity, I was leading my child to be someone who I hoped would do the same.

Spoiler alert: It worked!

NO MARTYRS, PLEASE

At no time has being a servant mom meant losing my sense of self—this isn't about being a martyr. I was committed to it from the depths of my heart, even when my feelings of inadequacy created immense self-doubt. However, I soon realized that leading from my heart was the path to best serving my child. It's where I would stay, rooted in my intention to be of service. Moving from the heart means I'm listening, not only to myself, but listening to God as it is here that He lives.

For me, there is no contradiction in the message of servant leadership and mothering, as serving is a fundamental mission of both. To move from the heart, listening and learning means we long for the best for our children. I'm not talking about being the perfect mom, since there's no such thing, anyway. I'm sure God laughs at our pursuit of perfection, even as He accepts us as perfectly imperfect. As servant moms, we try; we stay open to possibilities and know that our imperfections will provide opportunities for lifelong lessons. This is true for our children and us, and embracing imperfection means we accept ourselves and our children as they are, unique imperfect individuals. Our servant motherhood style embraces this uniqueness and encourages us to help our children share their gifts with others.

Servant motherhood also includes the commitment to fulfill your role without seeking gratification and recognition. The proof is in the pudding. Gratification comes from what you have achieved. Recognition will be in the form of the light that you and your family contribute to the world. As we seek to serve by leading from the heart, love, goodness, and goodwill flourish around us.

All in all, my desire was to raise a confident woman, strong in her faith, and filled with passion and conviction to make an impact on the world in her own, authentic and lovable way. I prayed for her to be acknowledged and validated for who she was from the inside out. Unleashing my daughter into the world with strength, integrity, and compassion has been the culmination of my role as a servant mom. That was all that truly mattered to me. I loved or should I say, love my role as mom and would repeat every day of it again. I learned about myself, I learned from my daughter, and I learned to live and love as a servant mom moving from the heart. And as we seek to serve, rather than be served, we strengthen our capacity to lead from the heart.

MOM MEMO
What Is Servant Motherhood, Anyway?

- Servant mothers lead from the heart, which means helping children develop and grow—and soar along the way.
- Servant moms make it a priority to understand their inner journey, their strengths and weaknesses.
- Effective servant mothers persist and do what is necessary to find help to heal their own broken places and unravel issues from the past that could interfere with their servant motherhood journeys.
- Servant moms listen and learn to find ways help their children be the best they can be despite challenges and setbacks.
- An effective servant mom looks out for the best interests of her family, but is never a martyr; a "servant mom" never discounts her needs or puts herself last.
- Faith-inspired servant moms develop confidence and compassion because they seek spiritual guidance through prayer and contemplative time; they know they're never alone.

The greatest among you will be your servant. For those who exalt themselves will be humbled, and those who humble themselves will be exalted.

—Matthew 23: 11-12

TWO

Becoming Pregnant

Life is not measured by the number of breaths we take, but by the moments that take our breath away.

—*Maya Angelou* , Author-poet-actress

Would I someday become a mom? Of course, for most women entering into a marriage, having a child is a rite of passage. Indeed, I felt that call when I took my vows, especially because I'd always longed for a family of my own with several kids in the mix. Growing up in a solid Irish and Italian Catholic home, we were all about family: kids, cousins, aunts and uncles, second cousins and all those once and twice removed. This family piece of the puzzle nuzzled in my head and my heart.

As a faith-filled woman, my belief in procreation left me excited at the thought of starting a family. I was so ready to share the love in my heart. Becoming pregnant was *supposed* to happen when we were ready. Right? So I thought.

Fast forward and the well-known script seemed to play out according to plan. I married my childhood sweetheart, an officer in the U.S. Navy, and also pursued my career. Courtesy of the military, frequent moves were a part of the first few years of our marriage. At the start of year three of this military commitment, we finally landed a three-year tour in New England. However, circumstances unfolded for me very early in my marriage, when I realized I'd married my best friend. Love existed from a place of respect and admiration but our emotional and spiritual needs were so different that we were simply lacked the necessary compatibility to create a harmonious life together.

During the first few years of the marriage, I struggled to be the wife I told myself I needed to be. I put effort into trying to make it work, knowing that I had "a good thing." Although intimacy was minimal with time apart and lack of connection, we were still working on our marriage. Although we'd been open to starting a family from the beginning, three years had passed and I was not yet pregnant. I began to wonder why I hadn't conceived. One obvious answer rested in our military lifestyle. My husband was on shift work, and then out to sea for half of our short-married life.

My brain was also in overdrive, leading me to think that God might have other plans for me. Since my heart was still confused about my marriage, perhaps I wasn't supposed to have a child. I was uncomfortable with the current state of my body, questioning my fertility and my potential to conceive. The next logical step was to pursue a fertility conversation with my OBGYN. On my first visit, I was given what seems to be the first step for most want-to-be moms, to monitor fertility markers for the next two months. Because I wanted answers, I was diligent and committed to the process. I kept a calendar and recorded the requested information.

After following the doctor's directions for the next month, I returned for my second visit, by myself, because my husband was out to sea. I admit that feeling alone was familiar to me, as this is how I'd felt most of my life. But I was sad to be taking on this fertility issue alone. After nervously waiting in the reception area, I was called to the doctor's office, where I presented the charting "handout" previously provided. After reviewing the chart, he looked up, tossed the paper over his shoulder and compassionately said, "That's why infertility isn't a strict science. No two bodies are the same, and they don't follow a roadmap when it comes to conception. We have no answers at this point."

My heart sank. *But I'm a woman. I'm supposed to get pregnant. What does this mean? What next? Now what?* Feelings of failure and inadequacy surrounded me. Tears streamed down my cheeks. I left the office feeling even more alone than when I'd entered, and I desperately wanted to share the results of this first appointment with my husband. In those days, the only option was a *family gram,* a set word count message that would get bleeped across various, often unknown oceans and seas for your loved one to read, along with everyone else—there was no privacy for deployed military personnel in that era. Feeling ultimately alone and isolated, I sent the message. Looking back now it's difficult to believe the many significant events I endured by myself without the support of family or my husband. This was to be a consistent theme. I wish I could have reached out to my mother, but that was not the kind of relationship we had.

A TIME OF ANTICIPATION

Two months later, my husband returned from duty. We had a happy homecoming with time alone while awkwardly readjusting to our life as a couple. Struggling to connect and wondering what was next, I continued keeping myself busy and distracted as a youth minister, high school teacher, and fitness instructor. A few weeks passed. One day, while I was teaching, I felt "off" and wondered if what I was experiencing were signs of a pregnancy. The symptoms prevailed: nausea, tender breasts, exhaustion. But the timing of my so called "fertile" window and my husband's arrival home didn't match. Pregnancy wouldn't be possible, at least according to my homework chart.

I went ahead and scheduled an appointment at the military hospital for an HCG blood draw, a pregnancy test. I arrived at the hospital with a plethora of feelings in my body and in my head. My relationship with my husband, the infertility challenges I had been facing for three years, me a mom, were all spinning in my mind. After the blood draw I headed home to await the results, and a short time later, I received the call. I wasn't pregnant. Seriously? I shared the news with my husband, who was also disappointed by this news. I continued to wonder if this would ever happen. Regardless of my struggling marriage, I was praying to know I could conceive.

Another week passed but I kept my sadness to myself. Although I still felt sick, I continued to show up each day to teach the students and classes I enjoyed so much. After sharing my symptoms with a few of my female coworkers, they were convinced I was experiencing signs of pregnancy. With a slight ray of hope and a bit of hesitancy, I called my husband and asked him to pick up a pregnancy test on his way home.

That evening, I read the directions and prepped myself to take the test the following morning. I went to bed with my mind nervously racing.

Sunrise couldn't have come soon enough. Timidly heading to the bathroom, I took the test and went back into the bedroom to wait the few minutes it takes to see the results. My heart pounded and my palms grew clammy. I'm sure much of this emotional turmoil was related to the quandary I was in over my life and love and marriage. As much as I wanted a child, was I ready? Was I capable? Where was our marriage going? Ten minutes never felt so long.

The minutes slowly clicked by and it was finally time to check the results. Cautiously I peeked into the bathroom like an intruder. The tile floor was cold on my bare feet. The test seemed to be taunting me from the spot where I'd left it near the sink. Afraid to get too close I squinted enough to see a color change on the test that would indicate a positive pregnancy. *No way*. The test was positive. "Oh shit!" I said, my voice dropping. "I'm pregnant." That was my immediate, somewhat confused response. My husband, who was in the bedroom, nervously waiting to hear the results, said, "You don't sound too excited."

Frankly, I was in shock, nervous and surprised. My mind jumped to what was reeling in my life at that time. Factually, the timing, the math, and my cycle had been far from creating a perfect storm to become pregnant. What followed was a surge of thoughts around years of empty answers and attempts to conceive. Many women who have traveled this road understand that it is a lonely path of heart-wrenching head games of why me, what's wrong with me, and the notion that I was somewhat of a failure for not being able to conceive. Last and most important, I struggled with emotions surrounding a questionable marriage. What had been working in my head most recently was that pregnancy was not God's will for me. God's will is not our will. And so now I was pregnant.

Within minutes my mind switched to the notion that I had life inside me. Inside my head, I heard my doctor's words that fertility is not a precise science. The pregnancy test was confirming what I'd been feeling physically. For me, this conception was a miracle. If you looked at all of the scientific factors around the timing in which I could have, should have conceived, this wasn't the "right time." That is why I was convinced I wasn't pregnant, even when I wasn't feeling well. But God had another plan for me, and I knew this in my heart.

My eyes well up even today knowing that I'd been blessed with a baby girl, one God had specifically blessed us with—and me, as a mom. I quickly thanked God for this "miracle." I turned from nervous and fearful to ecstatic and knew I would love my baby from this day forward. I was going to be a mom.

GOD'S PLAN UNFOLDS

I share this story in part because I hoped to have a bigger family. I struggled to conceive again but it never happened. I believe God had a purpose for me to experience the joy of being a mom to a beautiful baby girl who would teach me lessons every day of my motherhood. And I'd experience the majority of this motherhood journey as a single mom. Many women have taken this journey from being a daughter with a mom to now being a mom with her own daughter. I wouldn't change the road I traveled for the world. With support from her dad, Kate has healthy family relationships on all sides, and is a thriving adult. I'm thriving, too, and the lessons from that day forward are still providing learning opportunities. How blessed I am!

You and I. Hand in hand. An endless story of love. A love that grew in me for nine months and only grows bigger each day.
—Veronika Jensen, Author-poet

THREE

Emotional Connections

You are my sun, my moon, and all of my stars.

—E.E. Cummings

When Kate was only 10 days old, her dad, a naval officer on a ballistic submarine, departed for his first three-and-a-half-month deployment. A ballistic assignment differed from an attack submarine in both the length of the deployment and the surface time. For example, an attack sub remained submerged for varying lengths of time, but surfaced throughout their tour in different ports worldwide. This allowed for time above water, a walk on dry land, and a phone call to loved ones. On a ballistic submarine tour, once submerged, the submarine remained under water for several months at a time. At the time, the family gram was the primary vehicle for communication between the crew and their families.

This was the era before cell phones, the Internet, and before personal computers were commonplace. The family gram was basically a paper form with thirty small rectangular squares, where we wrote one word in each square. Using the family gram was like a puzzle or a game in which the object was to see how much we could say using the fewest words. The messages were as cryptic as they were concise. I'd begin drafting a message on a scrap of paper as a practice form. Then I'd count the words, whittling away at them while still attempting to share the essence of happenings at home, including updates on Kate and anything else—in thirty words. It took some doing. It was difficult to craft a heartfelt message while remembering that the contents weren't private but transmitted by multiple unknown fingers across the world and into the deep blue seas.

After giving birth to Kate, I spent the night in the hospital with her. Her dad held her for an hour or so and then had to leave for a weekend of Navy tactics training before deploying. I know it must have been so difficult for him to say hello to Kate, only to then say goodbye. The next day, while packing up to head home, a nightshift maternity nurse came into the room to say goodbye, but also to give me some advice. "Your little girl has her days and nights mixed up. So far, she's a night owl," the nurse said. "She was wide awake all night and is sleeping soundly now that it's daytime. Hang in there as you attempt to flip that schedule around."

My in-laws, who lived an hour away, stayed with me overnight and sure enough, like most newborns Kate was up crying throughout the night. With everyone pitching in to offer lots of rocking and cuddling, Kate finally slept a little while.

The next day I was on my own. I was happy about being a mom though, so I accepted the new routine, or rather the lack of one. I stayed in the moment, embracing all that this journey brought with it, my own journey as well as Kate's.

My family was over 650 miles away and my in-laws about 60 miles from me. Naturally, I was a little rattled as I thought about my new life as servant mom. I felt so unprepared. God was my rock. I prayed for the strength to remain open to learn. I sought confidence and was determined to love intently and move with intention from my heart. Having strong faith means acting on something we haven't experienced yet putting trust and faith in God. This was surely a first time experience. I stayed hopeful that all these elements would ease my insecurities.

That first evening I stuck to the plan I'd devised for late night feeding in hopes that Kate would sleep through at least a few hours of the night. I wasn't breastfeeding, so I knew exactly how much formula she was consuming, which I thought might help me gauge what she needed to sleep for a little longer. Well, I got that wrong. Within a few hours Kate woke up and the crying began. I sat up in bed and waited to see if she'd fall back to sleep right away. She didn't. As a new mom I couldn't handle too much crying, so I jumped up from the bed and went to her. Snuggling Kate in my arms, I headed to the recliner rocker in the living room.

Rocking establishes an easy rhythm that often calms babies even if it doesn't put them to sleep. And I have to admit, it calmed me as well. I hummed lullabies and alternated the rocking with walking in circles around the house, hoping she would drift off to sleep. The nurse was right. Like many babies everywhere, Kate didn't know day from night.

RUNNING ON EMPTY

This pattern continued for weeks. Kate's night owl syndrome would begin around 1:30am each night. A part of me took a nonchalant approach to this. After all, what do babies know about circadian rhythms? Besides, I was so in love with Kate I'd have done anything to keep her comfortable. Still, I was anxious, nervous, and alone. I reminded myself that I was assuming the role of both dad and mom. Without my husband there, I had no breaks and no one who could take over a feeding or help with a diaper change. No other person was there to offer comfort to our crying baby. My natural enthusiastic energy began to wane as I suffered night after night of broken sleep, or at times, no sleep at all.

Although I tried to flip Kate's night owl cycle, the routine continued. Cry. Wait. Then pick up Kate for a middle of the night or wee hours of the morning feeding. Then it was back to her crib or perhaps the rocking chair or maybe in bed with me. To be honest, I was afraid to have her in bed with me. So many visions of mishaps and squishing her went through my head. If I did put her next to me, I didn't sleep anyway. A bassinette in the room was a possibility but her room was across the hall in our ranch-style home, so I could hear everything.

I'd put her down, then I'd wait again. That was the routine. At times, I'd stare at Kate in wonderment and love. How was she not collapsing of exhaustion, just like me? She slept like a champ during the day. I moved her out into the living area to sleep amidst the noise and daily routine. I even vacuumed around her and she never budged. All of this was evidence that her internal clock was still off. As each day passed, I attempted to facilitate her conversion from sleeping more at night, just as she did during the day. And each day I thanked God for this blessing, asked for continued patience, but also prayed for Kate to sleep and for the fortitude to keep going, even as I was running on empty.

EXHAUSTED MOMS

What new mother has not experienced these feelings of exhaustion? Maybe even with each new baby. I also prayed for strength to overcome the feelings of inadequacy, feelings I now know are not only normal, but ordinary. Now, I wasn't aiming to be perfect. I only wanted the ability to meet my child's needs, and there's nothing quite like fatigue to bring on a sense of inadequacy and doubt.

Within a month of giving birth I started working a bit from home. This was by choice, and there was no pressure to do so. Although working from home is more common now, it was quite unusual at the time. I had taken time off from my job as Youth Minister but was able to work from home when I was ready. Being alone, this was a healthy diversion while Kate was sleeping. It gave me the chance to feed my creativity and remain a part of community outside of this sort of isolation.

All of this was contributing to my increased sensitivity—and I didn't need that. I'd definitely define myself as an empath. As the weeks passed, I was predictably stressed out. I cried more easily too. By the time evening rolled around, even if I tried to bottle up my anxiety, my desperate prayers were about maintaining my energy and figuring out how to help my child sleep. With my emotions raw, I prayed for patience because mine was wearing thin. Of course, my motivation was simply to do this mom thing the right way. I was a rookie, learning not only about my daughter, but also about myself.

By this time we had a daily routine, which wasn't the one I'd expected. I tried to take occasional naps during the day when Kate slept. Working from home had its advantages, but it didn't solve Kate's sleep issue. Personally, I was never much of a napper but it soon became *my thing*. I learned the hard way that sleep deprivation is a real issue. Although family was far away, I did have my family of choice, my church family and friends. But they weren't around at bedtime. I had no option but to keep up without daily help or a substantial break. I got that! Or so I thought.

ASKING FOR HELP

One evening, Kate began her night crying, and I realized I was in for another sleepless night. I warmed the bottle and took her to our favorite rocker. As Kate nursed on the bottle, I fought back tears. Loneliness and helplessness settled in my tired brain and body. Taking a break halfway through the feeding, I sat Kate up and patted her back to coax a burp, and bam, there it was. Suddenly, Kate jolted and she projectile vomited halfway across the room, hitting the fireplace and scaring us both. I gasped. Kate cried. I comforted her as my heart raced while I reached for paper towels and prayed to understand what happened. I was so shaken I called my mother-in-law in the middle of the night. I was desperate for a bit of reassurance and comfort.

My mother-in-law's subtle words of advice calmed me and enabled me to think clearly again and settle down. Kate was fine. But what about me? Well not so much. I felt more inadequate than ever. But, I also realized that amidst all the turmoil, which I knew was normal new baby behavior, the nurturing, loving desire to make things better never overwhelmed me. I continued holding Kate and singing to her as we rocked and walked. When her tired body began to surrender to sleep, I laid her in the crib and snuck off to bed myself.

Within thirty minutes she was awake and crying again. I managed to get my weary body out of bed, and I lifted her out of the crib and headed to the rocker. I was exhausted, but she, on the other hand, was bright-eyed and bushy-tailed. I turned Kate around to face me, propped her up and prepared to have a conversation with a three-week-old baby. "Look my sweet child," I whispered, "it's just you and me. I need you to sleep. Days are days, nights are nights, so can we figure that out together? *We* need to rest." Emphasis on *we*. It was another long night.

. . .

HELP COMES IN MANY WAYS

The next day my parents called to ask how things were going. After sharing the challenge of a night owl newborn, my dad asked if he could give me a piece of advice. I welcomed any help at that point.

In a gentle tone, Dad said, "Listen Ritalee [my dad's name for me was "Re" and then he creatively added the "lee"], don't pick up Kate with any tension or anxiety in your body. She will feel everything you feel. Take a deep breath before you go to her and get rid of any tension. You're not going to help her if you're uptight."

Most of the time, suggestions and advice from our parents come and go. We forget some, remember others. But I never forgot Dad's advice that night. He grabbed my attention, which influenced the way I thought about parenting and my parenting style for years to come. Like the best messages, it was simple but powerful. My dad seldom dished out "long form" advice, the kind that are lectures delivered from a position of authority or power. Instead, he shared simple, direct statements or used metaphors or stories to make his point. And he always hit the nail on the head.

That night I got Kate ready for bed with my father's words playing over and over in my head. I'd thought I'd been holding and feeding Kate from a loving and a tension free space, even though I acknowledged tension and anxiety in myself. I quickly learned I couldn't pretend to be free of stress when I wasn't. Dad's advice helped me become aware—even painfully aware—of my breathing, the adrenal rush, my muscles contracting and relaxing, my heart rate, and more.

Without fail, Kate was awake at about 2:00am. I felt like Bill Murray in the movie "Groundhog Day." We had our own rerun streak going. This time, though, as I climbed out of bed I intentionally released any expectations, said a prayer, took a cleansing breath, and expressed gratitude for Kate. Then I made my way to her room. I reached down and enveloped her in my arms, now a stress-free place.

Our routine went on, but gradually I learned to relax and accept the situation physically, emotionally, and mentally. I believe Kate sensed the change in me, because she cried a little less and I became more patient. As the nights continued, I stayed true to our routine: A late night feeding, rocking and lullaby, then into her crib. As always, she slept briefly, woke up crying, and we repeated the ritual. Over time, after a few motherly tips from my sister-in-law and mother-in-law, along with my growing confidence, I let Kate cry a little longer over the next few nights. A few nights into the new strategy, I decided to let her cry even a bit longer. At times I had to cover my ears in order to tolerate the crying even for a few seconds, which felt like hours. Of course, my body tensed and my heart raced. As moms always do, I asked myself if I was a bad mother for letting her fuss just a bit longer. I so hoped she'd cry herself to sleep. *Just a few more minutes.* Deep inside me I wondered if she was *a high needs baby,* meaning physical contact was necessary. Either way I didn't need a label to decide if I'd pick her up…or not. She would not be at this stage forever. Kate would only be in my arms for so long and I wasn't going to miss loving on this baby whenever possible.

Ironically that night after this period of restlessness and my intermittent tears, we both fell asleep in our own beds. I awoke at 6:30am in a panic, convinced something had happened to Kate. I sprang out of bed and ran across the hall to her room, only to find her fast asleep. She'd slept through the night at four weeks old and never went back to being a night owl. Here I was, a parent alone praying for help, and God answered. This experience also bolstered my confidence that understanding and monitoring my own stress level would make a difference. Over time, I got a lot more practice, which helped me embrace more self-care in my servant motherhood role. "Don't you pick that baby up..." my dad had said at the beginning of his sound advice. How profound that statement was for me.

Many of us remember feeling the periodic or chronic stress and tension in our childhood homes. I learned to be tentative in my moves and interactions because the environment was stressful. I was, as therapists say, *vigilant*, reading the room, so to speak, and modulating my own behavior to avoid conflict. At times, the mood and high intensity made me anxious and uneasy, and I began to suffer intense migraine headaches at age eight. They lasted into my adult life. As a child I didn't know that the migraines, at least in my case, were largely the result of a stressful home life, a desire to please, and my dubious attempts to keep the peace. (I say largely, because I realize migraines have many physiological causes for those prone to them.)

Naturally, as a result of the tension, I experienced in my childhood home, I was committed to creating a stress-free atmosphere in our home. That meant working to establish our home as a safe and loving space. My garbage was not hers, and I wouldn't project it onto her.

So my advice is this. First, give yourself permission to feel. Check in with yourself and embrace your emotions rather than deny them. You're experiencing what you feel—it's real. Maybe you need some deeper work to recognize where these emotions are coming from and how to deal with them if they keep reappearing. But remember, your feelings emerging from the past are not your child's baggage, they're yours. Don't pass it on.

STRESS AND BAGGAGE

I learned a great deal about stress as I unpacked my baggage from childhood. First, as I examined my past, I identified stressors in my life. The thing to remember about stress is that it's a perception of a circumstance, not an objective reality; therefore, a situation that's stressful for you might not bother me at all. It's all in the way we see things. For example, let's say we're together in the car and I'm driving. The heavy traffic and speeding cars might be stressful for you, but maybe I drive in rush hour every day, so the traffic doesn't throw me in the least. Or, maybe you are so used to being the driver, you'd be stressed as a passenger no matter what. On the other hand, being a passenger doesn't mean extra stress for me. Same traffic, different responses.

Learn what stresses you, and then notice how you feel in various situations. Is your heart racing, are your fists clenched, is your breathing shallow? Maybe you're taking quick, short breaths? Headaches, poor sleep, overeating, or not eating at all, and drinking too much alcohol are common signs of stress in our particular era. As we all know, stress can lead to unhealthy choices and these choices also can affect our children.

We all encounter stressors on a daily basis, so for a healthy life we have to face them, which is why we need to learn what causes our individual stress responses. If you're having financial problems, look for information to help you cope. At the very least, or better, improve your situation. The same is true for anything related to your health, your work, or your family's difficulties.

Find ways to have time for yourself, whether it's a walk, reading a book, time with friends, or getting a massage. Bring your feelings of inadequacy and your frustrations to God in prayer. Let go of the ideal of self-reliance. So often we have a vision, then rush to figure things out on our own. Hoping to prove we're self-reliant, we convince ourselves that we are going to fix our issues alone.

It's kind of like the advice Faith gave me about getting in the boat and rowing. Although I embraced the "I can do it" attitude, I knew if I put the paddle in the water alone, I would not get far. We think that we're helping God out by just taking care of things ourselves. Looking into the Bible, we can read lessons of many who have tried to take matters into their own hands and failed. Moses, Peter, Jonah, and Paul all failed at one time or another. Paul teaches us about faith and demonstrates that our past does not have to define our future. The truth lies in patiently waiting to hear God's help, His direction for us. Pray for patience and the strength to let go and listen. Based on my Catholic faith, I often pray to the Blessed Mother Mary for strength and the ability to just listen to God speaking to me. She is an amazing role model for many women—and those of many faiths find Mary a helpful spiritual figure to turn to.

WHAT STRESSES YOUR CHILDREN?

In addition to acknowledging the stress other adults around us experience, we need to understand what our children perceive as stressors. Your career change or a move to a new home might seem like a dream come true for you, but your child might find the situation stressful, yet not be able to say so. Maybe your new job disrupts their routine. This can be as simple as the time they expect to see you leave and come home every day. If they act out in some way, assume they're stressed and hold their feelings in high regard. It might take only a simple explanation to relieve something that concerns them. You can also watch for signs that your children are putting pressure on themselves to perform better in school, to fit in, or to express themselves.

Some children hold up a false standard of perfection and then are stressed about not meeting it.

My early experience as a stressed-out mom with infant Kate taught me a great deal and also helped me think ahead to confront and address my concerns about my baggage. That was my path to finding help to create a new way of handling life's tensions.

As a servant mom, I created a "stress-handling model" for Kate. That involved assessing what Kate saw when I seemed upset or stressed. What was my body language communicating? How did I react—or appear not to react? By handling my stress, I could be sure I didn't lose my cool over an accident or a situation that could become a crisis. I reminded myself about the anxiety I'd felt in my home as a child, but I also repeated the advice my dad so eloquently shared with me. Was I approachable? Was I accepting and loving even amid stress? Those were questions I asked myself and prayed about.

As a single mom, I set the standards, values, and expectations for Kate, but the responsibility is the same for two parents, who must work through these issues together. For example, as a servant mom I took care to relax my standards around perfection. Attempting to live up to another person's—or society's—standards can be stressful for adults and kids. I've seen mothers burn out when they try to keep a perfect house, be a fantastic cook, excel in their jobs, look good, and be a perfect servant mom. Wow! Don't waste time trying that. It won't work. Unfortunately, it can be hard for some of us to embrace the fact that we can't do it all. However, with humor and a dose of reality you can ditch the myth of super-mom and embrace the concept of servant mom.

SELF-CARE ISN'T OPTIONAL

My career in the wellness industry had given me copious information about self-care that is useful in my work today. Through training, teaching, and many life experiences, I found ways we can put ourselves at the top of the to-do list to promote our overall wellness. Fortunately, it's not about money or having loads of time. Self-care is a lifelong journey to care for ourselves, no matter how pressed for time we are. It doesn't have to take a lot of time, especially when you're juggling all your jobs in a day, but it takes *something.*

Look at it this way, self-care sends a powerful message to your children. Making time for yourself says "I am important." This is a critical message for future dealings with other people, but even as they grow up they're likely to say the same thing about themselves and run their lives accordingly. Self-care can mean many things, but it's definitely linked to managing and relieving stress. For some it can include relaxation techniques, meditation, or simply time alone to walk or sit and enjoy the quiet of a room or a garden, or maybe a park bench in the city. Of course, it also means exercise and good nutrition. The ultimate message of self-care is letting go of control, a step in the right direction to relinquish self-reliance.

I recommend time for prayer as the foundation of your self-care. God knows you're busy but patiently waits through your busy day to have a few minutes alone with you. So, show up exhausted and speechless, but show up. Just be, sit and listen. That is prayer enough sometimes. With faith and hope we learn to let go and realize we are not in this alone.

QUICK STRESS RELEASE EXERCISES

Use the breathe-in quick stress management techniques. Sometimes, taking a few deep slow breaths will reset your immediate mindset—the present moment. Deep breathing is handy when you face a long line and are pressed for time, or your children are squabbling... again. Or your newborn is crying at night. Take a deep breath and exhale, and then take another, then another. This breath will help you relax before dealing with the stressor.

If you still need to refocus and let go of the stress, you can add a short visualization exercise. Try this:

Visualize a wall rack with a few hooks on it. Think about what is bothering you, stressing you out, irritating you right now, and mentally reach out and grab onto it, then visualize hanging it on one of the hooks on the rack. Leave it there—maybe for good, or perhaps to be addressed later. See yourself clean, clear, and ready to hold and embrace your next steps. Or maybe you're relaxed and now ready to go hug your sweet child.

MOM MEMO
Emotional Connections

- Stress is part of life, but part of our jobs as servant moms is to learn how stress affects us, because stress can be contagious. When we're tense and distracted, our children sense it and internalize our stress.
- Consider the source of what especially causes your stress. If it comes from your past, then it's your baggage, not your children's. It's up to you to deal with what's troubling you.
- Do you know what stressors your children face? Maybe they're afraid to "fail" or disappoint you. It's possible a

positive or negative change or shift in your life is stressful for them. How can you relieve their stress?

- Are you or your children trying for the unattainable goal of perfection? If so, relax that standard for yourself and make your children know that you—and God—do not expect perfection.
- Self-care, that is, treating your well-being as a servant mom priority is a way to be a positive role model for your children. Make time to relax and spend time alone or doing something you love.
- You deserve breaks, and time to maintain your health and wellness through exercise, meditation, or prayer.
- When in doubt, hug your kids. Everyone is happy when they're hugging.

Motherhood is not a hobby it is a calling. It is not something to do if you can squeeze the time in; it is what God gave you time for.
—Rachel Jankovic

FOUR

Pass It On—Trust & Sharing

You think you are just a drop in the ocean, but look at the ripple effects one drop can make.

—Unknown

If you've ever experienced a deep desire for something, you can relate to the anxiety, fear, and excitement that often attaches to a goal. You likely keep your eyes on the prize, as the saying goes, and your commitment to reach this goal—this desire—is unwavering. When we commit, then staying the course is not only doable, it's non-negotiable. Once the goal is reached, the desire fulfilled, we hang on tight to keep it close as if to protect and shield it from any potential harm or corruption. Sharing this goal may be a challenging proposition to even consider. But what would happen if you shifted your perspective? What if the worth, value, and purpose of your goal means even more when it's shared with others, strangers and acquaintances alike? This is how I felt about the birth of my daughter.

Shortly after Kate was born, my husband had to leave for his four-day submarine missile tactic training. The military waits for no one, and duty called. I distinctly remember him holding Kate, less than a day old, for such a short time in the wee hours of the morning with his departure only a few hours away. Still in the hospital bed, I quickly realized I was going to be solo in my servant mom role. Although Scott had asked the captain to be excused from this duty, the request was denied. Ten days later, Kate's dad would begin a two-year submarine tour, gone for three and a half months, home for three months. Repeat.

"You and me, kid," I said to my newborn girl. I held my baby girl tight after feeding her, in awe of this beautiful gift. Reacting like new mothers have for eons across the globe, I was amazed with the intricacies of the tiny human. I studied her fingernails, grasping their detail and the long, beautiful fingers. I placed my hand to her chest to feel her rapid heartbeat. Its meditative rhythm caused me to reflect on this wonder of life in my arms. Her eyebrows complete and detailed. Her nose, her eyes, her ears, all perfect. My attention shifted to all that was happening on the inside. All systems go on this first day of life. I was lost in my new awareness of the true miracle of life.

By the next day, word had spread that my baby had arrived. Working as a youth minister meant loads of parishioners and kids were waiting for this child to be born. So at times, when I thought of being alone as a new mom, I actually wasn't. There was a plethora of love and support around at all times, including a large group of teens taking part in our lives. Their enthusiasm awaiting the birth of this child was often quite exuberant.

Procedures were slightly different than they are today. In many hospitals newborns weren't necessarily in the room with their mothers during the first 24 hours. I'd had intense labor and a few complications, so rest was prescribed. Since my husband had to leave and my immediate family was out of state, I had plenty of reasons to feel isolated.

That afternoon, I was resting in my room while Kate was sleeping in the nursery, when one of the nurses on the maternity ward stuck her head in my room and asked, "Are the teens that just arrived yours?" I looked puzzled, because she added, "Fourteen teenagers are staring through the window smiling at your daughter." With a barely discernible grin, she paused and shook her head. "We only allow three visitors at a time." Oops. Now how did they get in here in the first place? I chuckled to myself.

Within minutes, I could hear the gentle murmur of youthful voices in the hallway, and then a group of excited teens crowded the doorway. They'd come to welcome Kate into the world and soon filled my room with their joy and excitement, laughter, and giggling—but not for long. A nurse soon appeared and nudged them along like a bunch of kids on a playground, reminding us all of the three-person max visitor policy. Naturally, that many teens couldn't be completely quiet. As they left they shouted congratulations. "Welcome Kate. We love you. Can't wait to hold you. Love you both," and on and on. Kate was as much a part of their world now as they were of hers. My heart was full on so many levels.

Within minutes of their departure, I was overcome with a moment of grace and clarity. My baby, like your children, was here to be shared with the world at large. This had a deeper meaning for me than just the obvious. Even as Kate recovered from a difficult birth journey herself, I knew she wasn't only mine. Her presence was a gift from God, but that meant balancing the parental possessiveness and control necessary to protect a child and preparing her to go out into the world one day.

The tendency to hold children close emotionally and physically is both required and normal, but it can also transform into an unhealthy need or desire. When the teens left the maternity ward after their visit, I had a clear vision, that moment, in my hospital bed. It was an intense faith-based directive coming from deep within me. I clearly heard the message: *This child is to be shared. Let her love and gentle heart affect the lives of many, and let others share themselves and what they have to offer with her.*

These thoughts reinforced my desire to raise a confident, loving, and strong child who would bring joy to others throughout her life. From that day forward, I had purpose and clarity in my mom role. However, I was about to find out that this could only happen by building my own confidence and strength as an emotionally, spiritually, and mentally strong woman.

Wanting to live as normally as possible during the months I'd be alone with Kate, I headed back to Sunday mass when she was about two weeks old. We were immediately joined in the pew by a few youth group members. A little later, I felt a gentle tap on my shoulder from the pew behind us. A family friend asked to hold Kate. I didn't hesitate to pass my new baby from my arms into hers. My heart was touched knowing we were already spreading and receiving joy and unconditional love through a cuddle or two. I took comfort from my calling to let go. "Share," is what I heard, I felt, and I knew.

THE CHURCH COMMUNITY SENDS A MESSAGE

Attending church on Sundays over the next few months helped me find support, but it also helped me nurture our family of choice. Because I remained open to sharing, and because I knew so many families in the parish from my work there, eager sets of arms and big hearts open to accepting some "baby love" were always available. Many loving arms held Kate during that time, but I wasn't worried. Members of our faith community were sharing themselves with my daughter. Sometimes I'd listen to hear a cry or baby babble as my cue to look around for Kate. But equally often, I'd hear nothing. During mass when I looked for her, it was not unusual to see she was on the other side of the church. Passed from one set of arms to another, Kate was becoming familiar with these faces—a good thing in itself.

As Kate became a toddler, she began picking and choosing her audience, which is part of normal development. I'd know she was on the lookout for those she could coax into taking her to the donut table after mass. She was on a mission. One Sunday after the liturgy of the mass, Kate, who was on her way to the donut table, was approached by three older women. These women enjoyed a bit of love and attention from this blonde-haired, blue-eyed toddler, and they gave it back to her. As they commented on her curls and smile, Kate was in a rush to get to the more critical piece, the donut. She rushed by, barely stopping to smile. I wasn't far behind, and I thanked them for their compliments and attention.

Later that evening at home, I believed I had a teaching opportunity for Kate. In words appropriate to her age, we talked about the simple pleasure that others, in this case elders in our faith community, received from a few minutes of shared attention and interaction with young children like her. I wanted Kate to learn that she had nothing to fear from becoming acquainted with family friends and parishioners who were part of our family of choice. I encouraged her to remember to take a moment to acknowledge individuals who speak to her and who like to spend a moment or two with her. She was too young to understand that she would also benefit from her interactions with these other individuals.

TRUST VERSUS FEAR

It's essential to teach our children to trust, and that includes all its meanings and contexts. As a servant mom, I realized early on that my child's first point of reference about a trusting relationship was based on the one she had with me. Through my actions, commitment, honesty, and truth, I provided Kate with a foundation she could use to gauge other relationships against ours, which offered a path to understanding how her future relationships could be built and maintained. It was also critical that Kate see the relationships I fostered were based on trust. If a relationship in my life was not honest, I ended it.

Our children are watching. As parents, we mirror for our children what is acceptable and what's not. In this book I've talked about trusting your instincts as a mom. Instincts play a legitimate and significant role throughout life, which is why we need to encourage our kids to pay attention to their instincts. As a parent, I wanted Kate to be polite and respectful, saying hello or acknowledging a friendly greeting from someone passing by. This was easier for young Kate to do when we were together, and as she matured, she formed the habit of being pleasant and courteous.

Equally important, I also wanted to teach Kate about awareness of her surroundings and to trust her innate sense when something didn't feel right. This is one of the most difficult parts of parenting today, and maybe for all time, but our children need to know it's okay to walk away from a person or situation that makes them uncomfortable, uneasy, or fearful. In other words, if something feels off, embrace what you feel and turn away. We have emotions and gut reactions for a reason.

Because we know it's impossible to protect our kids every minute, we must give them tools to defend themselves. Fear is an emotion. Appropriate fear coupled with confidence about what to do if someone behaves in an inappropriate or threatening way is a gift we can share with our kids, just as we share trust in healthy, nurturing relationships.

Remember, too, that we don't need to teach a child to *feel* fear. Our limbic system is the seat of our ability to experience all emotions; it's part of the human brain structure. Every emotion is a gift that sends a message and helps us evaluate and understand what's going on around us. However, what we *can* teach or pass on is a fearful attitude, or a fear response to a whole range of unknowns. That's where needed balance comes in.

I tend to think the best of people rather than the worst, but that attitude or stance doesn't mean I'm not cautious. As a servant mom, I had "the talk" with Kate. In her case it was about stranger danger, one of many realities kids face today no matter where they live. She understood that these potentially harmful situations could occur anywhere, even at school or at church. Communities face all kinds of potential threats, some more acutely than others, and "the talk" varies accordingly. But in every case parents are called on to walk fine lines. For example, Kate understood the concept of something not feeling right, regardless of who, what, or where, but at the same time, I remained conscious of not instilling unhealthy fear or paranoia, either. Yes, a fine line, but in today's world, a necessary one.

As parents, we're aware that our children encounter strangers all the time, but judging others harshly or becoming fearful and wary of people we don't know is an unhealthy place to live and plants seeds of bigotry and hate that divide us. That was not the way I wanted to raise my daughter. And from a servant's heart, I tried to avoid judgment without cause while at the same time teaching Kate discernment and ways to navigate in her surroundings that kept her both open and safe.

My trusting relationship with God provided a sense of peace and protection, but this didn't allow me to avoid teaching or modeling discernment and walking away, as well as building trust. As a single mom, I encountered situations in which I had to ask a stranger for help, or drive hundreds of miles alone at night and stop in unfamiliar places for emergencies or necessities. There were times I was the stranger someone else needed help from. This required an ability to assess situations and use common sense as I approached. In these and other situations, I always prayed and asked for a hedge of protection around my daughter and me.

As part of teaching discernment and balance, I encouraged Kate to talk about trusting God. To do that means knowing Him, not to just know of Him. Any relationship is a two way street, and my relationship with God is no different. We speak/pray, we listen, then discern and move with confidence. I know my prayers are heard, and I never walk into any situation alone.

Let your child see your trusting relationships and find confidence in God while nurturing a servant's heart that recognizes that we're all strangers somehow. As part of your balancing act, you can also focus on your kids sharing a bit of themselves with others in a safe environment and allowing others to do the same. When I think about trust and sharing, a particular couple, Mary and Wilbur Emerich, a warm and endearing grandparent-like couple at our church, comes to mind. With a soft spot for service, they were the first to volunteer to serve pancakes for family breakfasts or to volunteer for the Easter egg hunt for the young children.

Mary and Wilbur grew up in an orphanage, fell in love, and married for over 60 years. Although they didn't have kids, they enjoyed moments when they could act in a grandparent-like manner in our parish community. Kate benefited from their love and generosity, mostly in the form of time and attention. I still smile thinking about the uncomplicated communication the three of them had during a few moments of shared interaction.

When we moved away from that parish, I missed that Mary and Wilbur. But as I looked at the guardian angel picture in Kate's room, a gift they gave her when we moved, my heart filled with gratitude. A simple moment in time, a moment to pause, created a mutual exchange that had a lasting impact.

Even as a toddler Kate grasped my story about having time for others. Without having the vocabulary, she understood the idea of seeing the face of Christ in others. Her understanding of this concept grew, and the parishioners were modeling that principle by taking time for her. This early exposure to a range of people, like the Wilburs, helped me avoid instilling a universal or generalized fear of people they didn't know, not a negative concept in itself until we label people "strangers." Research also backs up the idea that children who are part of a community, such as a church or a day care facility or a preschool often are less fearful of others than those who are pulled away from the "unknown."

Of course, I'm not advocating for being careless about threats. However, I'm recommending that our children be allowed to interact with others in a safe environment. Their interaction may be as simple as a meaningful hello or working side by side on an outreach project to help those in need. As Christians, Jesus has told us to take care of others and that means giving our time and attention. It's not optional.

Being a confident mom comes with challenges, and at times it seems everyone around us has no problem telling us what to do. This is why throughout this book, I've advised you to dig deep to find trust in yourself and in your children. It's part of our job to not only allow our kids to venture into the unknown and conquer fears but to encourage them to do so.

THE VALUE OF OPTIMISM VERSUS THE ROLE OF FEAR

One of our jobs as parents is to help children develop discernment and learn how to navigate situations unique to their lives, but that doesn't mean we can't also be optimistic about our children and their lives. Early in Kate's life, I realized that if I had fear lingering from something in my past, I needed to face it and not project it onto my daughter.

Most of us were taught, to one degree or another, to adopt a fearful outlook or attitude in some situations, and we've used it as a reason not to do something. Most of the time, when we face one of these avoidance fears head on we realize that there was nothing real underlying the fear. I guess we could say the space was empty.

Aside from the fear of danger and threat, servant moms can also teach our children to use fear as a tool to help them try something new rather than avoid it. In other words, our kids can learn to use fear to support an optimistic approach to a new challenge or an unfamiliar situation. In fact, rather than avoid fear, help them examine it and look for the energy and learning potential present when fear shows up. Discernment is often misinterpreted as discovering the dangers in order to not take action, rather than using the same set of skills to discern and then go ahead and take a chance.

WE CAN AVOID TRANSFERRING FEAR

Many kids learn to ride a bike with some coaching by a parent or older sibling, and the time it takes may vary, but it's a commonly learned skill. Let's say, however, that you remember having huge fears about riding a bike. You're fine now and cycle all over town, but still, check that old memory at the door. Most kids learn the skill without undue fear, and your child is likely one of them. Teach the basics, including the safety regulations you insist on, but beyond that, let go.

Listen to yourself as you offer advice, maybe overdoing it just a tad...be careful on the hill, watch the cars, avoid the stones on the path...and on and on. Now, each situation is different, and as a parent you know the hazards unique to your environment. Perhaps the first time your child leaves the bike path or the sidewalk and ventures into the street, a "pop quiz" on safety might be in order. In other words, rather than delivering a litany of advice and reminders, let them tell you what they know about that steep hill or the traffic. Remember, your kids are aware that wearing a helmet or the need to navigate around the ditch are *facts, not fears*. Then, knowing they're well trained, wish them well, say a prayer, and send them on their way in your characteristic spirit of optimism. There's a big difference between saying goodbye to your child with, "Have a good time," versus, "Be careful...watch the traffic...peddle away from strangers..."

Of course, I, too, understood the possibility that my daughter might feel fear when traveling into the various "unknowns" she'd encounter even while living a faith-based and optimistic life. However, I also had to deal with my own fears so they wouldn't unfairly influence decisions I made in raising Kate, or project fears I'd once had onto her. After all, if we let it, fear can find its way into most every area of life. From meeting new people to embracing an academic challenge, I wanted to create an environment that cultivated a spirit of discovery and adventure that includes being willing to take chances. Of course, I was protective, but I named and dealt with my fears and made intelligent, sensible, and cautious decisions based on the facts I had at the time. It was important to learn about and heal my insecurities to avoid transmitting them to Kate.

As servant moms, dealing with our own fears before we pass them on to our children is part of our role in developing resilience in our children. This theme of resilience runs through many chapters of this book, and it turns up here once again. Observing your trepidation in certain circumstances and examining the origin of your fears is a necessary step. If you see your children worrying, talk to them about it while watching how they convey their hesitancy around a situation or a person. What is the black hole they fear? Is it something that perhaps *you* fear? If so, make an effort to release it.

Releasing my fear of letting Kate go, even as an infant, and sharing her with others and allowing them to share themselves with her, was a major step in building her inner security. I saw the value for our kids when they spend time away from parents. In Kate's case, she spent time with her Dad, grandparents, cousins, and other relatives. She took trips with friends without my fear standing in the way or posing endless "what if" questions.

In my prayers and quiet time I often reflected on the first two days of Kate's life, when I knew my purpose was to share this child and let others share themselves with her. This is how she developed thoughtfulness and compassion, attributes I was proud to see as she matured and ventured into new, exciting experiences.

Early on in Kate's infancy, a friend reminded me that each day of our new child's life is a step closer to independence. Our nursing baby eventually moves to a bottle and then a cup. They move from a swaddled lump of love to rolling over, to crawling, to walking and then getting their driver's license. I'll never forget the day Kate got in the car by herself after passing her driver's license tests. I watched her walk out to the driveway and get into the car and drive off to school. My heart stopped, but I knew she was just experiencing another step toward independence.

Speaking of independence, after graduating from Xavier University in Cincinnati, Ohio, Kate pursued a Masters in Communication Sciences and Disorders and was accepted into a program at the Massachusetts General Hospital Institute of Health Professions. This was exactly the program Kate wanted and had gone after, so it was an exciting time. However, her program began three weeks after graduation, which meant she had to quickly find a place to live and get her bearings in a new city. Kate and I quickly worked to find a small apartment she could rent in a Boston suburb with access to the public transportation system, known as the "T."

The T was a new experience for Kate, and she admitted to being both excited about figuring out the routes and such, but simultaneously apprehensive about being thrust into that part of big city life, especially after four years at Xavier University, with its small community atmosphere. Now she was a newbie, essentially alone. Fortunately, Kate had her strong faith to rely on as she used her discernment skills and overcame her fears and navigated through her new life with all its routines and demands.

I'd be lying if I claimed I wasn't nervous about Kate leaving the relatively safe environment of her college campus and venturing out and living by herself for the first time. I prayed every day for her protection and success in this new chapter, but I sometimes lay in bed at night thinking about her comings and goings on the T and in her new environment. Ultimately, though, I didn't allow "what if" thoughts to occupy space in my mind and seed growing fear. Instead, I prayed and asked guardian angels to protect and watch over Kate.

Kate's adventure had its challenges at the onset, but she soon found a great group of friends and enjoyed her program. She moved into a house with three other young women and thrived in Boston, earning the degree that had brought her there.

Throughout motherhood, I was reminded of this launching responsibility I had, fully aware that I was not doing this on my own. I had prepared, protected, and prayed over my little girl, presented her to God, then let go, knowing she would be in God's hands. Sure, I experienced some grief and sadness when Kate left the house for college. It felt like a nanosecond that Kate spent at home. I'd miss her voice and all the noises associated with a teenager in the house. But she was now stepping out to create her own life.

PREPARING FOR THE LAUNCH

Passing infant Kate around to others in the church was somewhat of a metaphor for realizing that she wasn't going to be in my physical presence or in my care forever. She would be launched into the world on her own. Likewise, a servant mother's responsibility lies in creating a foundation to launch confident, compassionate, heart-centered individuals into the world. Kate taught me this lesson when she was only an infant. What I learned when I turned around and didn't see this child right behind me in our safe environment was that someday she'd be on her own, affecting the lives of others in what I prayed would be a positive way. She was not only a gift to me, but a gift to the world.

Keep in mind that the lives of our children affect us and our families, but also the community as a whole. I like the way Lutheran theologian and child development specialist, Professor Marcia Bunge, explains our children as gifts:

Children, we should remember, are God's gifts not only to their parents but also to the community. They are members of a community from the start, and they play various and complex roles within it. In addition, they will grow up to be not only sons and daughters but also husbands, wives, friends, neighbors, and citizens. Viewing children as gifts of God to the whole community radically challenges common assumptions of them as "property" of parents or "economic burdens" to the community. (Marcia J. Bunge, *Rediscovering the Dignity and Complexity of Children: Resources from the Christian Tradition,* 2004.)

MOM MEMO
Pass It On—Trust & Sharing

- Stand back, use your discernment skills, and then let go of fear and share your children with the world and likewise, let others share themselves with your children. This is how they develop kindness and empathy and understand shared purpose and joy.
- Deal realistically with the realities of today's world, assess situations that could pose threats to your children, and teach them ways to avoid those situations or handle them if they occur.
- Deal with your own fears in order to live in a positive, optimistic light and pass that attitude on to your children.
- When our children live without fear, they can freely and joyfully interact with others and be willing to take chances to enrich their lives and share themselves with others.
- Listen attentively when your children express fear about something. Deal with the causes of their fears to help them see many of their fears as opportunities to act.
- Help your children understand that the stance or attitude of fear sets up barriers to meeting new people

or trying new things, or it can lead to excessive worry and anxiety.

- Letting go of fear is when the magic truly happens and the world opens up.

"The Lord bless you and keep you; the Lord make His face shine on you and be gracious to you; the Lord turns His face toward you and gives you peace."

—Numbers 6: 24-26

FIVE

Graham Crackers & Milk

In the end, kids won't remember that fancy toy or game you bought for them, they will remember the time you spent with them.

—Kevin Heath

In the sixth grade, I broke my wrist doing gymnastics. After receiving an X-ray on both wrists, I was sent home with what was diagnosed as two badly sprained wrists. Still in extreme pain, I sat at the kitchen table that evening attempting to eat something—anything. I didn't have much of an appetite. My mom gave me a glass of milk and a plate of graham crackers. Sprained wrists or not, I was able to dunk graham crackers into a glass of milk. That was the medication that eased the pain, at least for a little while.

We soon learned the X-rays had been misread, and my right wrist was actually fractured and required a cast that went up my arm and down my hand. Somehow, I still figured out how to dunk and enjoy those graham crackers.

One night when Kate was in elementary school, she got ready for bed, and the two of us said our prayers and sealed our day with a goodnight kiss. A couple of hours later, I headed to bed myself, but had a difficult time sleeping that night. It appeared Kate was having the same trouble because even from down the hall I could hear signs of restlessness in her room. A few minutes after midnight, I heard her voice. "Mommy, are you awake?"

"Yes, and so are you. What's the matter?" I asked. "You can't sleep?"

"No," she replied.

"I have an idea," I said, still in bed. "Do you want to meet in the kitchen for graham crackers and milk?"

Of course, I was met with a resounding, "Yes!"

"I'll race you to the kitchen on the count of three. One, two…"

In a flash, she was out of bed and got to the kitchen first. Barefoot and dressed in our pajamas, we grabbed our goodies and took our spots at the table. I left the lights somewhat dim as we shared our graham crackers and milk, along with conversation and laughter. In that moment, our enjoyment of our spontaneous kitchen meet-up was clear to me, and the spontaneity of our midnight escapade held the attraction for Kate far more than the graham crackers and milk. She giggled with excitement that the moon was out and we were up eating graham crackers and milk.

I never forgot that moment of exquisite connection. The struggle for a connection at home was a theme deep in my heart during my childhood. Feeling emotionally secure is the path to connection; likewise, connection is an integral part of emotional security. You can't truly have one without the other.

Like many adult women, I'd learned how to silence many of my feelings, usually after calculating it was the way to avoid bad feelings or tension with my mother when we were going through some unrest in the family. On top of that, I wanted to be met where I was in the moment, perhaps upset or preoccupied with something I wanted and needed to share. However, emotional availability was limited at times, so I'd often keep my tears and emotions to myself.

I believe the ability to communicate without fear is essential between parents and children, because it leads to ever deepening connections. The ability to communicate starts early, and it doesn't have to play out only in stressful situations, but is equally valuable during the delightful "graham crackers and milk" moments. Moments like the one I shared with Kate keep the doors open. As we know, small children start down an interesting communication road when they begin the steady stream of "why" questions, which prompt answers, followed by more and more questions. At some point, though, children reach ages when they open up fewer conversations, and soon their impulse to communicate seems to wither and fade. Talking less or not at all is a potential hurdle we parents face, and when that happens, we might sense the connection our children have with us is weakening.

KNOWING WE MATTER

I didn't need a counselor to tell me that children need to know they matter. Still, in counseling, I was led to contemplate the depth of that statement. More than anything, I wanted Kate to *hear* that message from me, which I then supported with my *actions*. That meant spontaneously delivering the message when she still was a young child. I'd lower myself to my knees to be at eye level with Kate, reach for her hands and say: "You can always count on two things in your life. Our home will be filled with love and laughter, and you will always know you are loved."

I showed that love through communication and connection. That's what sharing graham crackers and milk in the kitchen was all about. It sent a message that being with Kate was my priority—that above all else, she mattered. I missed a certain amount of that connection piece growing up, but by becoming aware of it, I stayed open to pursuing common ground with my child. This intentional openness to Kate emerged in what I came to see as my role as servant mom.

I've relished the ritual that continued to develop over time. The conversations started with Kate as a young child laughing and embracing her dunking snack at any time of the day. As Kate matured, our conversations intensified over a variety of subjects, from school to friends to hardships and, of course, personal victories.

WASH, RINSE, REPEAT

The graham cracker ritual soon became a mother-daughter thing for us. It morphed into a significant gesture of communication whether Kate was four or twenty-four. Kate was very young when the graham cracker ritual quickly became "our thing," but I didn't necessarily have expectations it would continue on through childhood and into her young adult years. However, I eventually identified what made our ritual a great bonding, connecting moment. First, there was a wash, rinse, repeat quality to it we could count on. Our treat was never consumed standing up or when we were rushing around. Instead, we gathered the crackers and always placed them on a plate. We reached for the proper glasses and thoughtfully poured the milk as we got ready to dunk.

Part of the value of maintaining our ritual was in recreating the atmosphere and attitude of open-hearted space. It was a time Kate and I could laugh, cry, share stories, and enjoy the uninterrupted time. My childhood memory was now taking on a life of its own with my daughter and for different reasons. Of course, its importance went way beyond sharing a snack.

WHAT MIGHT YOUR RITUAL BE?

It doesn't take much effort to create a bonding ritual with your children. It doesn't have to be based around food; ours just happened to be. Pay attention to all kinds of opportunities to form an even deeper connection between you and your children. No matter what, stay in the moment and observe what comes from these moments. Perhaps your moments or rituals involve a place, or a song, or a book, but whatever it is, it will be unique to you and your kids. Tuck away the opportunity in your toolbox and you'll have it to pull out and use in a lighthearted spirit of fun and relaxation.

If you need a chance to connect, your son or daughter will be touched that you remember the elements of the special moments. Then, years down the road when your kids have families of their own, you may see this "thing" you created repeat itself with the next generation. This is one more way to let your child know you were, and still are, paying attention to what connects you. It's your "I love you" gesture, yours and yours alone, and has benefits beyond the content of the ritual or action itself.

THE ART OF LISTENING

By showing up day after day for Kate, I learned what listening was all about. As nurturers today, we're usually on the go. We know (or have told ourselves) we must do it all. Almost all of us juggle numerous projects at once, no matter if we're in the workplace or are a fulltime parent and homemaker. We can't find enough hours in the day to get it all done. This was true for me, while at the same time I wanted to be approachable and attentive as I developed solid pathways for communication with my daughter, regardless of what was going on in my world.

Enter the art of listening, something I found challenging. I had to work on it constantly. I first became aware that if I asked the question, I needed to be ready to hear the answer. Remember the saying: "God gave us two ears and one mouth for a reason." It makes sense. Talk less, listen more. Got it. So, the first principle was to actually listen to the answers to the questions I posed.

You might wonder how you can do this in the midst of a stressful day, when demands are coming at you from all sides, and each child needs your attention. Here's the reality: *If we want to develop listening skills, we have to put distractions aside.* Multitasking is not a sign of success. As a mother, you'll always have a running "to-do list." In my experience, I had to declare that my list didn't matter, at least at certain times. I learned to stop, put the next string of demands aside, pull up a chair, and listen. That meant focus, eye contact, actively listening and hearing Kate's story. I learned to pay attention to the feelings—the emotion—coming through the story. I listened for an underlying current being revealed in her wording. Whatever the scenario, though, I learned to stay present and absorb the content of the conversation. Equally significant, I listened for what was *not* being said.

Since I never wanted to assume anything, I could phrase open-ended questions that encouraged and allowed for greater detail, and I always hoped, self-expression. I wasn't perfect, mind you, but I began to see the art of listening as a critical skill for a servant mom.

CREATING THE SPACE

I also learned to set aside time to create an invitation to share. I didn't need to pencil these into the calendar or set reminders on my phone. I created space in the kitchen as I made dinner. Now and then, I turned away from the cutting board or turned off the stove so I could listen for a few minutes. Perhaps it meant closing the computer screen and physically moving away from distractions at my desk. We can silence cell phones and text notifications, which, today, is a powerful message in itself. It says: "I'm here for you."

As a parent you must deal with endless distractions, not only for your kids, but for you, because rarely is anything so urgent you must turn away from a conversation with your child to pick up a text. Rarely must you either connect immediately or miss out. We even have an acronym for this, FOMO—fear of missing out. We should be asking ourselves, "Miss out on what?"

An environment that can be interrupted by the phone or texts or social media is by definition not a safe environment for communication. The person you're communicating with wants to be assured they have your full attention. That's why it's necessary to consciously and deliberately eliminate distractions at critical times. No one can be perfect, but to the extent you can, create a safe atmosphere for communication even if little or nothing is said. Sometimes you won't exchange words, or it may be that there are no words for the situation at hand, but just showing up can be a catalyst for communication. In other words, when your kids want to start a conversation, take them up on it. Be ready.

Although it isn't always necessary to create rituals around communication, or designate a space for your chats, doing so can help establish trust and common ground, which facilitate a receptive mood. Maybe you have a favorite café or diner, a picnic table in a park, or a walking trail. People often engage in easy conversation while they're in motion. Your special place could be cozy chairs in your favorite room. The kitchen was one of our spaces where sharing developed around graham crackers and milk. I had a particular affinity for those graham crackers because of my broken wrist episode. It was a memory that brought with it a bit of comfort and simplicity. Perhaps it was the dunking and eating that created an underlying nurturing element to it.

THE LESSONS I'VE LEARNED

As a servant mom, these graham crackers and milk sessions taught me several lessons. First, as part of other efforts to explore and heal areas of myself, I not only learned to listen, but I understood the value of that one gift I could give. It also helped me embrace the unique role I had as a mom. Every day was a step in preparing my child to be released into the world as an independent person responsible for her choices and directing her own life. That was my job and now it's your job. Simply sitting and being in the moment with Kate verified my intent to concentrate and heed what she was saying.

Learning to listen also meant learning to adapt to consciously making an effort to understand where my child was coming from. It meant keeping my perspective out of the conversation and turn to actively listening to what she had to say. Listening often means saying nothing. As a servant mom, it also was important for me to understand the context around the topic of the conversation. Observing body language and tone of voice, along with my ability to recognize and read feelings were part of listening. Oh, feelings, the mysterious element we as parents sometimes want to squelch or minimize. We may find ourselves afraid of our children's feelings. Are tears and "being emotional" seen as a weakness? I don't think so. Compassion and empathy come from the heart and for some they are expressed through tears.

Of course there are other emotions such as anger, fear, embarrassment—and more—that need to be shared in an accepting environment. With this also comes learning how to share emotions appropriately. As parents, we need to guide and teach our children about appropriately sharing what's on their mind. "Stuffing it," a term associated with keeping emotions and feelings inside so as to not hurt another person, can actually result in physical damage.

As a wellness professional, I'm well aware of the detrimental effects that keeping emotions inside can have on the body. Muscles have memory. The body is smart. Emotions that are tucked away when we refuse to deal with them manifest and emerge from the body in some other way. Headaches, sciatic nerve issues, or potentially serious illnesses can result from keeping it all inside. Emotions serve a purpose and when shared honestly are not to be considered a sign of weakness.

Throughout my journey, I remember talking about tears and emotions with my counselor Faith, who reminded me: "Feelings are feelings. They just are. They're neither right nor wrong." When I attempted to hold back tears, she encouraged me to let them go regardless of what I'd been told in the past. She also said, "Have you ever considered that your tears are one of your greatest gifts, showing empathy, compassion, and more?"

I'd never thought about it that way, but she was right. I've learned that my heart and my kindness were critical drivers in the servant life in which I believe I've been called. This work helped me embrace my emotions and open my heart as a servant mom, which then led me to be receptive, attentive, and in tune with my daughter's emotions in the moment. Tears or no tears, emotions come and go; it's up to us to pay attention.

CONSCIOUS LISTENING

Who doesn't want to be heard? I mean honestly heard from the heart? If we pay attention without distractions and allow our children to speak their truth, we can then reveal our capacity for empathy. Nodding your head and agreeing is way of showing understanding and sympathy as we listen, but this may only touch the surface. For example, it's almost instinctual that parents want to give advice and control the conversation and steer it to their desired outcome. Like all parents, I had to learn to let go of my expectations and show up for whatever that moment brought.

When it came to riding along for a conversation with Kate, the driver's seat was not mine for the taking. This is true for you as well. So, moms, hop in the passenger seat and enjoy the ride. It's your turn to listen with no backseat driving. It takes practice, but it's fulfilling to listen and hear from the heart. It can be awe-inspiring when your children speak and share a challenge, a dilemma, or a fork in the road and find a solution without you saying much. It means they worked it out and came to their own decision, and you were their sounding board. Those are the affirming moments of a servant mom.

SACRED SILENCE

Listening to the silence is as critical to a conversation as listening to spoken words. Being present and able to shut up means we embrace our child's thoughts or feelings instead of our own. We parents often have so much to say and share that we forget to listen to what is *not* being said. As we know, silence can be used to express anger or resentment, or can be misinterpreted that way, so we need to convey that's not the reason for our silence. You want to be certain your silence sends the message: "I'm here. The floor is yours."

Lulls in a conversation can feel awkward, but I advise letting the silent seconds stand. Even in your uneasiness, learn to embrace the pause rather than rushing to fill the space. It isn't empty space, but is silence, and it has meaning.

Set aside your perspective and experience the conversation from your child's point of view. Perhaps most critical, avoid becoming "mind busy," you know, formulating your response while you wait for your turn to talk. You run the risk of missing what's being delivered to you in your children's words.

A pause, or silence in your sharing, can potentially lead to embracing vulnerability. As a servant mom, I learned to share appropriate experiences and ideas from an authentic place.

It wasn't that I had all the answers, but I was sharing specific times of challenge, success, happiness, and fear in my own life. This sharing was about more than surface-level feelings. It was about honesty and vulnerability that come with sharing my successes, hurts, and failures.

INTUITIVE LISTENING

As a servant mom, I began to listen on a different level, one related to my gut feelings, my intuition. I would get a sense of what was brewing inside and pay attention to how my body reacted. I learned to lean in, embrace, and develop my understanding of intuition.

Over time, I increased my intuitive capacity and paid attention from the inside out. Intuition is a powerful tool. We all have some type of intuitive presence in our life. Its value to us depends on how we choose to both develop it and use it. Albert Einstein and Steve Jobs both attributed their success in life to intuition. Einstein said, "The intuitive mind is a sacred gift, and the rational mind is a faithful servant."

Embrace the ability to listen to the body and the intuitive messages it's sending you by way of your gut or other areas in your body. Sometimes we negate intuitive feelings, and perhaps go with external guidance that seems more authoritative or logical, but once we begin to trust our intuition, we will learn to trust its guidance. Certainly, some people have a more significant gift of intuition than others, but I assure you that the more you pay attention to intuition, the more skilled you'll become at understanding what it's telling you. Intuition isn't a whim, a product of the imagination. It's a gift. Lean in and develop it.

RELYING ON FAITH

As a woman of faith, I also have learned to listen to God. Even as a single mom, I knew I wasn't raising Kate on my own. My faith is the foundation of my life, and I move and direct my life's work from this solid ground. I brought my fears, anxieties, hopes, and dreams to prayer each day, but I also learned that petitioning requests and desires to God were only a part of my faith journey. Here, too, I learned to listen in prayer, rather than showing up with my laundry list of needs for God. The place where God speaks and lives in us is in our hearts. It is in quiet and silence that the Spirit moves. Comfort, direction, and simple peace happen in stillness. I know mom mode often means being on the go constantly. Carve out space to just listen and God will speak.

As a servant mom and servant leader, it's essential to develop contemplative prayer, which means staying quiet and listening to God while experiencing His movement in your life. For me this has meant long walks on a calm beach, meditating, or starting my day with a prayer ritual, or a gratitude journal. It's about asking the committee in my head to take a break rather than constantly telling me what I should or could do.

These actions have helped me develop a relationship with God, knowing it takes time, intent, and the perceived risk of trust, of faith. I brought my anxiety, fears, and challenges to the table knowing God wasn't judging me, but rather encouraging me to be a more robust and faith-filled servant mom. I trusted that my prayers were answered in God's time, not mine. That was not always an easy pill to swallow, but I remained steadfast and confident that God would provide—answering my prayers accordingly.

THE PAYOFF

As Kate grew up, we continued to create "bonding moments," but nothing replaced the graham cracker and milk opportunities. Age had no bearing on this and we continued dunking through middle school, high school, and beyond. Serious discussions took place, but we'd also unconsciously created a tradition that beautifully connected us. We shared this graham cracker and milk ritual when we wanted to talk, laugh, cry, celebrate a memorable moment, or simply share time. Kate was an independent, confident young woman in high school, which meant she had a full schedule. But we still shared many late nights at the kitchen table.

When Kate went to college, I struggled with empty-nest syndrome. I missed the noise and laughter that had filtered throughout the house. Of course, I missed our conversations and time together. But I was always ready for her next visit home. I kept a box of graham crackers in the cabinet, awaiting her arrival. She returned the gesture and kept a box in her cupboard when she knew I was coming for a visit. College stories and life-changing events led us to exciting and heartfelt conversations. Our time together mattered, regardless of the distance. Neither of us forgot our ritual.

After college and graduate school, and then beginning her career as a speech pathologist, Kate became engaged. During all the planning, I invited her for a mother-daughter spa weekend. Arriving before Kate, I entered our hotel room to stock the refrigerator with a few snacks and a bottle of wine to share. After Kate arrived and started unpacking she called out, "Mom, look!" Out came a box of graham crackers. A smile and hug said it all.

Even though Kate is a married woman now, we still occasionally share graham crackers and milk. Years ago, a good friend spoke of her adult relationship with her daughter and said, "We enjoy our children when they are young, but your relationship with your adult child is quite special, Marie." I would wholeheartedly agree with that as I watch Kate live her life. Somehow, I believe our dunking ritual will create even more magical moments in the years to come.

MOM MEMO
Graham Crackers & Milk

- Learn how to be a better listener than a talker. It takes work to hone this skill. Two ears, one mouth. Listen twice as much as you speak.
- Create a safe space for your child to share, embracing *all* they have to share without judging or having them fear being rejected.
- Pray. There are numerous ways to pray. Work on the same listening skills when communicating with God. Carve out time to sit, bring your day to God regardless of how it went, and once you have shared stop and sit in silence. God is speaking.

Listen to anything your children want to tell you. If you don't listen to the small stuff now, they won't tell you the big stuff later.
—Kevin Heath

SIX

Happy Unbirthday

Never stop showing someone how much they mean to you.

—Anonymous

Birthdays have always been a big deal for me. Even as a young girl, I woke up excited on the day. Sure, everyone has a birthday, but as a kid, I believed I was the only one born on that day. My parents kept a large felt board in our kitchen hallway, and one of the family rituals involved leaving messages on that board about holidays and special events, including spelling out "Happy Birthday" in felt letters for each family member. My grandmother was a teacher and passed the felt board on to my mom, so we had all the cutouts needed to celebrate every occasion.

I recall a few birthday parties where one or two friends came to my house after school. My first bike, a pink two-wheeler with an attached basket, was my favorite childhood birthday gift. The birthday child—or adult—got to choose a favorite dinner and homemade birthday cake.

Since birthdays are a big deal for me, starting early in my life, I remembered birthdays and sent cards to family, friends, and colleagues, and often called them, too. These days I might text or leave a voice message. Sometimes I mail a gift, or bake a cake, or even organize a birthday party. Birthdays signify our entry into this world, an event worth celebrating. Needless to say, nothing changed when I had Kate. Birthdays remained a big deal.

Kate was born in early January, although her due date was December 21. As much as I was ready to give birth at the 36-week mark, I also welcomed her delayed arrival, even speaking to Kate, saying, "Hold on, let's get past Christmas." And that's exactly what happened. I was admitted to the hospital, and my water was broken to start labor, and eighteen hours later Kate arrived.

As I've said, I had worries about being a mom, especially as I struggled with moving forward with my relationship with my mother. Somehow, it seemed a little ironic that Kate and my mom would share the same birthday, January 4.

Of course, no matter the date, Kate's birthday will always be special, a really big deal, but still, I was pleased she was born far enough away from Christmas and New Year's when so many other celebrations are going on. At some point, I decided to create another occasion to celebrate Kate, and the "Unbirthday," a/k/a "Katie Day," emerged. This was simply another "just because" reason to acknowledge Kate and say I love you in a different way. No guessing, no wondering, no waiting to hear it, no overkill, no spoiling, no helicopter parenting. Just honest, genuine love. (As an aside, I called her "Katie" when she was young, but in her teens she wanted to be Kate. I got that, but sometimes I still call her Katie. Seems many moms have a hard time letting go of the endearing little kids' names.)

Midway through the calendar year, I'd randomly pick a date for the official "spontaneous" celebration of Katie Day. Since Kate was quite young when this began, I didn't announce the day to her in advance. While she was still sleeping, I'd make signs that read "Happy Katie Day" and tape them to the wall in her bedroom along with balloons, a few streamers in the hallway, and other signs in the kitchen.

The plan was for Kate to choose from her list of favorite things to do and we'd plan the day around them. I often had a pretty good idea where we might end up. On the morning of Katie Day, I went into her room, and as she opened her eyes, I'd sing a made up little ditty and dance routine as I wished her Happy Katie Day. I began this tradition with Kate when she was three years old. The first time I surprised her, and she sat up and asked what Katie Day was. When I told her it was her day to pick whatever she wanted to do, that sounded great. But why? That was the part she didn't quite understand. I explained that I simply wanted to celebrate her—just because. "Is that okay with you?" I asked. "It doesn't need to be your birthday to celebrate you, right?" She eagerly agreed.

After a "Katie" breakfast, Kate chose the itinerary for the day. The library was first on her list of favorite places, not surprising to me because Kate loved books. Games, books, and listening corners made any library a favorite destination. She'd enter the children's section and find a cozy spot to settle on the floor near the shelves. Then she'd pull books from the shelves and begin reading or leafing through the pages to look at the pictures. Kate established a pile of the books she planned to take home, and another that she leafed through quickly and put back on the shelf. She could stay there for hours, and then when it was time to move on to our next destination, Kate marched up to the checkout counter with an armload of books piled to her chin.

This kind of independence in choosing books and knowing the procedure to take them home was a rite of passage for Kate—and for most kids who are introduced to the library early in life. After the library we'd head for the next stop on the Katie Day celebration.

A visit to the duck pond in a nearby village was also high on Kate's list. Like most kids, Kate loved tossing treats to the ducks, and she always made sure every duck in that pond got something. It was such a simple thing to do, and the joy on her face made my heart sing.

For lunch, Kate had a choice of bringing a picnic or heading to her favorite local restaurant. Later, we'd start to wind down our activities by creating dinner at home. We'd chat about the day and share the joy and laughter we found in the simplest things. The finale was a movie or a game Kate picked out, or we'd read one of the books she brought home from the library that day.

Although "Katie Days" began when Kate was very young, they evolved as she matured and continued on for years. The adventures changed as she matured, but the attention and focus of a random Kate day never changed. Over the years, the day represented the need to connect or was just an opportunity to spend time together away from the familiar environment. On occasion, I arranged for an overnight getaway so we could talk, laugh, and relax together. Along the way, Kate's favorite things included a spa day, a weekend at the beach, or a train trip into New York City for shopping and/or Broadway show. I often tried to keep the element of surprise, but as Kate grew older and our schedules and home-work life became more complex, secrecy wasn't always possible.

THE UNBIRTHDAY SPIRIT

These days given a special designation don't have to be as elaborate or costly as weekend trips or other expensive entertainment. Your child will understand limitations or what's possible for your family.

Unbirthdays or special "just because" days aren't about what you do, they're about how you feel. Lunch, a movie, a walk, or bike ride might feel special if you don't ordinarily have much time for these things. Or, a train ride to another town for lunch can be exciting for a child who's never been on a train. A joint trip to the mall's climbing wall might be what your older child thinks is a grand adventure.

As time went on, the beauty of Unbirthdays was that Kate began planning these days for me. One Christmas Kate handed me an envelope and as I unfolded the piece of paper, I realized she'd given me a "rebus," a puzzle that combines illustrations with individual letters. I'd worked through these types of puzzles as a kid. For example, the word "before" would be depicted by a picture of a bee, a + sign, and the number 4. You get the picture.

I enjoyed seeing Kate's creativity on display; half the fun was attempting to solve this puzzle in a room full of family. We laughed so hard we cried as I tried to "decode" this rebus puzzle made from magazines and downloads of web pictures.

After numerous attempts and some help, I learned my gift was a trip to New York City to see a production of "Jersey Boys."

Knowing that Kate found joy in creating a memorable "reveal" made it an even more unforgettable gift.

Christmas 2017

Mom

+

Kate

Train

to

NY

to

See

Jersey

+

Boys

on

!!!

Broadway!

NO REASON NECESSARY

My positive experiences with Kate reinforced the idea of celebrating children for no particular reason. I pass on the Unbirthday concept because unexpected and spontaneous surprises cultivate a message that you honor and love your children for who they are. When you dedicate time to connecting with them they understand how much you value them and your relationship. Sometimes, birthdays can feel "dutiful," and come and go with obvious regularity for every member of the family. It's the "just because" part that makes Unbirthdays special.

Children always want to be the center of your world, so setting aside a time for them sends a message that nothing matters more at that moment. As long as the activities fit your means, let your kids choose and lead the event. Then while you're having your day, at home or out, give them undivided attention —put the phone out of sight. Even if they're teenagers and they've already fallen down a social media rabbit hole, give them a taste of life without distractions.

No matter the age, you can replay that day's events for years to come. Fortunately, making memories isn't linked with expensive or elaborate plans. A lunch date, a hike on a nearby trail, or a walk in a new neighborhood fit the definition. I realize some of you have a larger family of kiddos. Still, I recommend making this Unbirthday or "just because" day happen, even if it has to be part of a day. If possible, make a day or a date with each child. Maybe you'll have only an hour or two to carve from your busy schedule to go out for dinner, a dessert, or a movie. Each child matters, but in larger families, sometimes kids tend to feel lost in the shuffle. At times I felt that way growing up with three siblings.

This date with an individual child is especially important if there are legitimate reasons one child needs more focused attention. In some cases, attending one of their sports events is special if you're unable to watch them play or perform regularly. Or attend their concert or robotics tournament and then celebrate their greatness for the remainder of the day. Sometimes, even in the midst of chaos, having days to celebrate a child's achievements or participation is a welcomed reprieve from everyday lives for moms and dads.

Even as time marches on, these days need to remain on the calendar. If need be, set a reminder on your phone for the next date or the next son or daughter's turn to celebrate outside of their birthday. Any opportunities offer potential to create parent-child rituals of sorts. That's why Kate and I still plan these special days together to leave other concerns behind and simply enjoy each other's company.

MOM MEMO
Happy Unbirthday

- If you decide to do an Unbirthday, create a workable game plan that will promote a connection and memories of one-on-one time that will last—it doesn't have to be elaborate or expensive.
- Do what's necessary to create even small opportunities to communicate to your children that they are the center of your world. Make these celebrations of your children happen—you'll never regret the effort.
- Keep Unbirthday or "just because" events simple enough that you aren't stressed and worried about being able to make them happen. These are supposed to add quality and fun, not add burdens.

- More important than anything else, use an Unbirthday to stay in your children's world—and in the moment.

Surround yourself with people who celebrate you. You deserve to be motivated, encouraged, supported, lifted, surrounded by love and celebrated.

—Pennie Hunt, Author and Professional Speaker

SEVEN

Forego the Agenda

I've learned that people will forget what you said. People will forget what you did. But people will never forget how you made them feel.

—Maya Angelou, Author-poet-actress

When I was a child, I did my best to avoid any number of unpleasant situations, and one that I avoided at all costs was being sick enough to stay home from school. The physical symptoms weren't pleasant, of course, but the consequence of staying home was missing out on all the activities related to school. However, far more significant, being ill meant being alone.

As one of four children, I shared a room with my sister and the boys had the other bedroom. We all got along well and entertained each other all through childhood, except when we were sick. While our siblings were off at school, we were tucked away in our room and left to our own devices, which meant entertaining ourselves. If luck was on our side, the portable television propped on its roaming cart might make it into our bedroom, but we had to be sick at home for more than a day or two to enjoy that luxury. I can't say for sure how sickness was defined in our house, but to get the extra perks, our illnesses had to be prolonged.

When I was in high school, I had a bout with mononucleosis, which meant being homebound for six weeks. That entitled me to an extended TV visit in my room—along with a tutor to keep me current with assignments so I wouldn't fall hopelessly behind. I've never forgotten the loneliness and disappointment I experienced during this "lock down." I was missing out on everything. I couldn't see my friends and couldn't participate in any of my regular activities. My disappointment lasted for many weeks after the diagnosis.

Like most moms, mine had a daily agenda and a to-do list that dictated most of our days, and hers as well, of course. Taking care of a home, four kids, and shuttling us back and forth to activities was a full-time job for her. For some reason I had a sense of the ever-present "always do" list, and not just when I was sick. This meant I often struggled to identify an appropriate time to interrupt. Time was scarce, and even more so when Mom was nursing a sick child.

Mom was a good nurse, so we had what we needed to get us on the road to recovery, but apparently, a few moments of solace didn't fit into the schedule. We might be stuck upstairs feeling rotten with a cold or whatever, but the world continued downstairs. The intent to keep the other five people in the house healthy was obviously wise, but that meant enforced separation, the main reason I hated being sick.

When I was sick enough to stay home, I'd hope Mom would spend a little more time with me by way of bedside attention, but that generally didn't happen. Staying in my room alone, not sleeping much and mostly having no television available, made for lonely sick days. I looked forward to the end of the school day so I'd have the company of my sister and brothers. Even as a teen and as a young woman, I still spent much of my sick time alone in order to stay out of Mom's way.

Later when I was a mom myself and had a sick child at home, I was hit with a rush of memories and beliefs about being sick. With a child of my own, what would I do when sickness reared its ugly head? First, I found that having insight into my own childhood, thanks to therapy, I was able to immediately switch gears into my natural inclination to nurture, empathize, and be in the moment. I wanted to be bedside and actively attending to my child. I was in mom mode, present and empathetic. Sure, overkill was possible, but I was self-aware, as I'm encouraging you to be, and I avoided the "hovering mom" scenario.

Putting our own children aside for a moment, it's not difficult to grasp the loneliness and sense of helplessness that come over us when we're sick. For me, tenderness, authentic concern, and the willingness to be interrupted showed up loud and clear. As a full-time working mom, I had a dilemma, of course, as most mothers do. Because I didn't have chronic health conditions and was rarely ill, I was able to use my allotted sick days to stay home with Kate when she was ill. If you have that option open to you then use it if you can. If you don't have paid sick days, the situation is much more difficult, for sure.

Whatever your circumstances, make a commitment to be as present as possible and offer as much attention as you can. Most of us want Mom around when we're sick. When Kate wasn't feeling good, she'd say, "Stay with me, Mom." Recalling my emptiness and feelings of loneliness as a child, I understood Kate's desire for a bit of TLC from me.

IT CAN WAIT

Like all mothers, I had an agenda, a schedule for a full day of events on my calendar, but if Kate fell ill, I knew in my heart, my plan for the day would have to wait. Being home with my daughter became my priority. I was honest with my employer that I was a single mom and would use my sick days to care for Kate if she was ill. I was clear that I'd first take care of Kate and then do whatever had to be done for work. During my years as a spa director, I had dozens of mothers on my team, some married, some not. Given my own situation as a single mom, I could be empathetic and flexible in working out ways to somehow get the work done. We found workable options.

Nowadays, at least for some women, working from home is an option and putting in extra hours on other days after the crisis has passed is another. In fact, the trend toward working from home may help ease the burden of caring for sick children in many households, especially for those with two parents. Regardless, during Kate's younger years, I figured out ways to do what was necessary to take care of her during the inevitable childhood illnesses.

The precious moments with Kate were irreplaceable. She would be a small child for only a short time, and I didn't want a sitter or caregiver stepping into my role as mom. It was important to create loving and nurturing memories for Kate around illness. No smothering or overbearing behavior emerged, by the way, only some extra attention and love. Many times she just wanted me near her when she didn't feel good. She'd stretch out on the couch snuggled in a blanket and want to see a movie, and she almost always asked that I sit with her. She'd even point to the other end of the couch as if instructing me where to sit.

I was happy to accept the invitation to join her, and my agenda went by the wayside. I knew where I was supposed to be, right there, right then, in the moment. Work would still be there the next day, but today's moment would be gone. When Kate fell asleep, I went back to my work, usually from the end of the couch.

When our children are sick, we'd do anything to take away their miserable symptoms. It's natural that we want to fix things and do the best we can to help ease their coughing, fever, or chills, but the most reassuring thing we can do is show up and stay in the present physically, mentally, emotionally, and spiritually. At times less is more, and the power of your presence includes the power of unspoken words. That's true in our dealings with any ill person, family or not.

LIVING THE MESSAGE

In my life with Kate we embraced the concept of taking care of the sick far beyond our own home. As Christians we're called to feed the hungry and sick and help the poor. Through my attention to her, I hoped Kate would pick up on the importance of embracing the needs of others, remaining selfless and empathetic to their needs. As an individual and as a servant mom, I was committed to embracing and living the concept of compassion for others. We can give attention and time to the sick through simple gestures like making soup for an ill neighbor or making a homemade card to leave at our neighbor's door.

Kate and I moved often as I followed new job opportunities, which meant we didn't have family close by. We could still share these acts of kindness with new neighbors, parishioners in our church, or our new "family of choice." We brought food to the homebound, made soup for the sick, and walked up the street to deliver cookies to our neighbor who'd just come home from the hospital. No matter where we moved, giving aid to the sick and suffering was a part of our life.

Parents often wonder if the lessons we impart to our children will stick when they're grown and on their own. So far, I've seen the values come to fruition in Kate. She has been involved in projects that called on her to be there for others and nurture those in need. First, she attended a college on a full-ride scholarship that included her commitment to ten hours of Christian service per week. She worked in halfway houses, clinics, and served underprivileged urban children. I witnessed Kate's love, compassion, and Christian service in action.

In the spring of 2020, amidst the rapid rise of COVID-19, my father was nearing the end of his life. Although my dad struggled with a few health issues, he didn't have COVID-19, but because of the pandemic, he couldn't see his doctors on a regular basis. So, it's fair to say that he didn't die of COVID-19 but COVID-19 didn't help, causing restraints in doctor visits and limited access to receiving timely medical information. No one had expected this sudden downturn in Dad's health. The COVID-19 restrictions ultimately prevented us from visiting him in the hospital, so as a family, we decided to bring him home with hospice care.

In what turned out to be Dad's last seven days, I saw a beautiful example of love and compassion. The concept of just being present, staying bedside and praying, singing, and nurturing my father was happening in full force. I watched Kate, a speech pathologist in the acute care unit of her hospital, give loving aid and attention to her grandfather. She was a natural and a source of comfort to her grandmother and me as well. But I also saw her struggle to keep it all together while feeling pain and sorrow herself. She was well aware that I was going through the painful process of slowly saying goodbye to my dad. I made myself available to her, just as she was doing for me. During this time with my dad, the nurturing element of being a servant mom emerged between Kate and me. Servant motherhood was mirroring itself in the comfort and love exchanged between the three of us, Kate, me, and her dying grandfather, my dad.

Throughout my years in the hospitality industry, I did endless trainings on customer service. One of the first questions I'd ask participants was: *Do you believe customer service is innate or trainable?* The response was always split, and many would argue that there's no one correct answer, anyway. Most attendees would say that it was innate, something that came naturally as part of an individual's personality. Others argued that if desire is present, a person could be trained in customer service.

I tend to lean towards the side that it is somewhat innate, that the desire to serve or be compassionate is somewhat of a gift. But when it comes to parenting or management, I do believe that our children and people we lead learn from our example. It's up to parents and other important adults to model the gift of sharing, the gift of compassion. These qualities allow us to think beyond ourselves. A compassionate heart shows itself through service for those who are less fortunate or in dire need of attention.

Kate was scheduled to return to work after a few days with her grandfather, but she made the decision to use whatever time she had to stay with him. She, along with our entire family, stayed close to my dad until he took his final breath. Kate showed a willingness to be flexible and put aside the proverbial to-do list and was fortunate to have options.

Sickness isn't planned, nor is a death or other kinds of family emergencies, so it's no wonder we cope with being pulled in different directions. When a critical moment shows up and a decision needs to be made to stay home from work, fly to a funeral, spend time with a friend or family member, this struggle hits home. As a servant mom, I went through times when I was afraid I'd disappoint my daughter, my boss, family and friends, and even myself. The to-do list always lingered and pulled at me in a way that seemed to echo "stay the course." But simultaneously, as a servant mom and as my own person, I longed to move away from the rigidity I vividly remember from childhood. Still, I knew I couldn't do it all.

ASKING FOR HELP

During my early mom years, I established a process I'd use when unexpected situations required a decision. I'd bring the concern to prayer, asking for wisdom and humility in making a decision. Through a process of discernment I was confident I'd make a decision that brought me peace. What do I mean by discernment in this context? Discernment is about the relationship between God and me. It means that I pay attention to a thought, a possibility, and where it comes from. Is it from my head? Or is it from my heart where God lives? I dialog, I pray, and most importantly, I create space for silence so I can listen to God.

Paying attention and using discernment skills means I strive to acquire a certainty about what comes from God. It's about learning to listen and understand God's ways, not our ways. It's about being open rather than being stubborn and thinking I'm right. Here I move far away from all the "buts" and distractions around the situation and ask, "Is it important to *you* to be there? And when I say *important,* I mean searching and deciding from a heart-centered place. Whether it was my daughter's bedside or some other place, I dig deep to listen to my heart. I also flip the question and ask, "How will I feel if I *don't* go?" (Or stay, or speak, or remain quiet...each situation is different.) And most importantly, am I willing to trust, even though I may not know the reward or purpose of this decision right away?

My walk of faith often takes me to a fork in the road. We may feel vulnerable after choosing a particular path, but that path is the place we are to be at that time. Your life is a series of decisions, especially when you're in the role of servant mom. However, we aren't meant to figure out what choice to make alone. Embrace the fact that God gives us directions for making wise decisions. We must take the time to pray about that decision, then let go and trust that God has a plan.

Sometimes we have to assure ourselves that even though the reward isn't imminent, we choose path X because we pray and believe it's the right thing to do. When my dad was dying and we didn't know how much time he had, I made a plan to make the ten-hour drive to be there to help my mother and family and to be at my dad's bedside. The day before I was leaving, Kate called and said, "Hi, Mama. [Her other name for me at times.] How would you like a copilot?" With both of our husbands flying out at a later date, Kate, who lives about 90 minutes away, offered to come with me. Her thoughtfulness in this tender time for me brought me to tears. I was beyond grateful.

Even when we arrived in Ohio, my dad's life expectancy was still in question. Kate planned to stay two days and fly back to Rhode Island, with plans to return later with her husband. As Kate was getting ready to leave her grandparent's home for the airport, she whispered to her grandfather that she was leaving. In and out of consciousness, he heard her and managed to mumble, "No." That brought Kate to tears. They were still streaming down her face as I drove her to the airport. "I don't want to leave," she finally blurted. She took a deep breath and asked me if she should stay or go?

Here we go again. As a mom, I wanted to provide love and support but not swoop into "I'll fix it for you" mode. I put my blinker on and quickly pulled into the last parking lot before the airport entrance. After giving her a hug and exchanging a few "what if" scenarios, I said, "You have a lot on your plate. When I encounter these dilemmas, I ask myself, 'Will I regret not being there when I look back on it in years to come?'" Then I added another observation. "You might be asking the wrong person because I look at these "once in a lifetime" opportunities and ask myself if any dollar amount could replace them?"

Kate made a few calls to her husband, her office, and to the airlines. She got off the phone and said, "I'm staying." Back to the house we headed. That was the decision Kate's compassion, flexibility and discernment skills led her to make. My dad passed away three days later.

INEVITABLE CHANGE

When the COVID-19 pandemic hit, we all had to adopt a new approach to our to-do lists and agendas. This was especially true for those whose children were still at home, but we were all required to make some changes. Flexibility and creative problem-solving tested every parental skill that exists. A certain amount of rigidity went by the wayside, along with regular routines and habits, as home offices and homeschooling became a new way of life for many parents and kids. I can't even imagine the degree of creativity and forward thinking required of every servant mom to accomplish these changes and keep life as "normal" as possible. The consequences of added demands and the economic and professional losses for women are still being evaluated and experienced.

Being adaptable and flexible without generating greater tension is such a valuable example for our children, who learn by observing. They see how to make the best of a last-minute change when a crisis hits, especially one with the urgency of a life-altering pandemic. When COVID-19 struck, plans and agendas disappeared. Kids visited grandparents on computer screens; high school seniors missed proms and in-person graduations. Sporting events were canceled, marriages and memorial services took place on Zoom, and our social lives ground to a halt. Even now, as I write this, we're still working our way back to regular interaction.

The pandemic was ongoing as it spread across every region and state, with surges coming in waves. Many parents lost their jobs and were forced to put their agendas on hold and use every bit of creativity they could call upon to keep their families housed and fed.

Flexibility was a more useful trait than rigidity, and many became masters of improvisation. In some ways, we reimagined regular events, and proms and weddings surfaced as backyard events. Some graduations were redesigned as virtual get-togethers or held with families in cars in parking lots. For the most part, adults and kids found ways to make the best of crummy situations that were particularly hard on children of all ages.

So, regardless of how you feel about your adjustment today, examine your response to the pandemic. What did your children see in you when life threw you a curveball? What example did you show to your kids, even your young adults? Your children were able to see their parents in action during a time when yesterday's agenda had to be scrapped to adjust to the unfamiliar demands of a global crisis. The pandemic hit every town and neighborhood in this country and across the world. It diverted our to-do lists and routines for what amounted to over two years.

Now it's time to take stock of what we learned about responding to the unexpected and our ability to put aside or changing our daily goals and agendas.

MOM MEMO
Forego the Agenda

- Give up the agenda and stay present with your child during an illness. Sit bedside or couch-side while they sleep. Being an arm's reach away is a message that will go deeper than you can ever imagine, both for you and your child.
- A day home from work could mean a productive day in the house, but forgo the to-do list, or at least part of it, to just be.
- Sit down, slow down, and convey the message to your child, silently or verbally, that this unplanned illness is okay. You are present heart and soul to comfort and cheer them back to wellness.
- Your message is a lesson. Nurturing, loving, and expressing compassion will foster a lifelong gift of empathy for those ill and struggling. It will clearly express and define the inconvenience and unpredictability of illness, but shows your ability to embrace the moment and selflessly deflect other distractions. This is a priceless lesson you will pass on to your young people.
- Trust me… your ability to be present will continue to work in the future, even with an adult child who needs you from time to time. Your loving, nurturing presence will remain both important and timeless to your offspring.

I tried to teach my child with books;
she gave me only puzzled looks.
I tried to teach my child with words;
they passed her by, often unheard.
Despairingly I turned aside;
"How shall I teach this child," I cried.
Into my hands she put the key;
"Come," she said, "play with me!"
—Author Unknown

EIGHT

Spontaneity: An Essential Ingredient

We learn to be spontaneous and free as we grow in self-awareness and self-esteem.

—Melody Beattie, from *The Language of Letting Go*

Structure and discipline are mainstays in my life. As an athlete and entrepreneur, I embraced the concepts of focus and a commitment to training, which required hours, days, and weeks stretching into years of discipline and structure. To reach the finish line, I had to be fully engaged and even rigid at times, while also being flexible when presented with alternative methods to help achieve my goal. Simultaneously, I heard the little voice in my head that wanted a little more spontaneity in my life. I had to work at really listening to it. Focus and discipline had blunted my internal freedom that would allow me to accept last-minute invitations or to juggle my schedule to make room for something unexpected.

I have distinct childhood memories of last-minute invites to gatherings. "Come over after church for coffee and drinks," a family friend might say to my parents after Sunday mass. Or we might receive an impromptu invitation to join a family for pizza or to go to a friend's house for a dip in the backyard pool. Most often, my mom said an abrupt, "No thank you." We four kids might plead and beg my mom to accept the invitation, but rarely did our pressure tactics work.

My mom kept a close routine as she organized our family and kept us under close surveillance. For her peace-of-mind she wanted to know our whereabouts at all times, and strict planning and scheduling was one way to keep track of us. I can hardly fault her for that—all mothers and fathers like to know where their kids are. However, as we matured through childhood, the answers to our "May I…?" pleadings didn't change. The familiar refrains were, "No, not today, another time," or, "You're not going today."

I noticed a pattern to the no answers as they related to my dad's business travel. With Dad miles away, being rigid and in control probably reinforced Mom's sense of safety. That's speculation on my part, but it's based on seeing the pattern. I don't believe Mom intended to disappoint us, but her refusal to change a plan or invite in something new, on-the-spot, got old. Meanwhile, my ability to be spontaneous faded fast.

When I went off to college, my newfound freedom intimidated me. True, some kids abuse the freedom that comes with starting college or career training or a full-time job. In my case, I became more reluctant and somewhat timid about being spontaneous. I met last-minute changes and on-the-spot invitations with trepidation.

It didn't take long for me to hit the pause button and reflect on the reasons why I was so reluctant to accept spontaneous invitations. More often than not, I found myself begging-off "because of my schedule." I soon realized that I had to be aware of this habit before I could change it. Once I was conscious of my pattern, I began to push myself out of my comfort zone. Ever so slightly I committed to being more flexible, saying yes more often, and not letting opportunities pass me by. That small step led to a deeper understanding of myself, and soon I was less willing to let my inherited rigid attitude detract from experiencing my life more fully.

In other words, in order to expand my horizons, a normal phase for young adults in their late teens and early twenties, I had to be less inhibited and fearful. I was motivated to change, because I had baggage and hurt attached to the outcomes when rigidity prevailed. But, easier said and all that. I was unsure of my relationship with spontaneity, although I heard the taunting, nagging internal voice that urged me to step out of my comfort zone and develop the ability to be responsibly flexible. My intuition was telling me my behavior was about more than simply saying no a lot. I started by letting go of my need to adhere to a set schedule, day-in, day-out. When I first began to say yes, I had to accept the uncomfortable, even slightly anxious feelings that come with change. At the same time, I practiced developing my inner freedom to say yes to new, spontaneous opportunities.

AVOIDANCE VERSUS SPONTANEITY

While I worked at unraveling my past, I recognized the safety net I temporarily created by saying, "I'm sorry, I can't." It was an avoidance technique related to fear, hidden deep down inside. I also experienced unexpected feelings associated with being spontaneous. Put another way, to embrace the unknown, we also need to develop our sense of security and confidence. Although I'm an extrovert and feed off the energy and inspiration of others, I've often shied away from impromptu change, while at the same time I wished I could be more of a "free spirit."

Before I could change my approach to spontaneity, I had to dive deeper and fill in the blanks about why I needed such a strong emotional safety net. I'm not alone in unraveling this kind of past. Children often construct a safety zone around them and learn from cues in their environment what is acceptable in the moment and what isn't. I believe I was afraid to act out verbally or emotionally, so I learned not to let go in the moment. As a child, when the unexpected happened at home, perhaps somebody randomly stopped by our house or one of us brought a friend home unannounced from the park across the street, then unrest and even panic resulted. Schedule changes and unexpected visitors could feel almost catastrophic. The actions and energy related to these events were difficult and embarrassing to witness.

Clearly, being financially careful and also responsible for my behavior from an early age, led me to almost automatically say no to spur-of-the-moment invitations or events that would challenge my preconceived notions of what I was allowed to do. I began college with student loans and whatever help my parents could offer, but in my sophomore year my dad lost his job. His job change had been the reason we'd moved from Connecticut to Ohio four years earlier when I was a junior in high school. My heart ached for my dad and the situation surrounding his recent upheaval. He gently approached me about the financial strain of continuing my education at John Carroll University. I was committed to staying, however, so I pursued jobs on and off campus to earn enough funds to make it work. Of course, my added commitments crushed much of my potential to be spontaneous. I had two reasons to say no most of the time, money being the first, limits on my time the second. Spontaneous adventures from a quick pizza party to a jaunt to a concert required money and time I didn't have. So, for some opportunities the decision to say no was already made for me.

In other situations, no wasn't an option. One of my jobs was that of Resident Assistant. As an RA, I was responsible for overseeing residence life in one of the dorms while living there myself. When the Assistant Director of Housing spontaneously booked a puddle jumper flight from Cleveland to Chicago for resident assistance staff, I couldn't say no. We were going to Chicago for a meeting and dinner before flying back that evening. With no time to think about it, I was thrown far out of my comfort zone. On the other hand, this spontaneous demand turned into an opportunity for some fun and laughter to come into my otherwise serious, focused life. I was jolted into confronting my insecurity around freedom and spontaneity. The fact that this incident stands out many decades later reveals its deeper meaning for me at the time.

I found it difficult to work through my discomfort around spontaneity, but I took steps to look at the dynamics and be open to educating myself about what it meant to have a degree of freedom. I needed to understand why I'd formed an association between spontaneity and potential danger. Expanding my life and saying yes, even taking certain kinds of risks, were part of a healthy lifestyle, which opened up the potential for greater creativity and the ability to embrace more joy and happiness in my life.

SPONTANEITY AND PARENTING

By the time I became a mom and worked through my childhood issues, I wanted to remove rigidity and inflexibility from my repertoire, while also maintaining guidelines and responsibilities for Kate. And yes, achieving that balance is a nearly universal quest for most parents. In my case, and maybe yours, it involved determination to stay in the moment, and sometimes it was advantageous to interrupt my routines. I was far enough along in my journey that I was able to embrace such moments with my daughter. These became times when we had a chance to enjoy each other and life. I soon realized these in-the-moment happenings had the potential to be cherished memories in the making.

Back in college I'd begun to understand the beauty of freedom, the value of setting aside rigidity and replacing it with possibilities. As a woman of faith, I also began to recognize the gift of grace in these moments. How beautiful that became over the years.

Embracing impromptu opportunities also entered into my alone time with God. Sometimes I'd feel a nudge to change my routine around prayer, even with Kate, and instead, listen and look to see where God might be showing up. At one time I adhered to my set schedule of rote prayer or my list of daily intentions, but the more I understood the value of spontaneity, the more I stopped to take a breath and notice God's presence in something outside of my plan. Perhaps it was embracing my surroundings during a walk on the beach or engaging in an act of kindness with Kate.

At times a nudge from the Spirit brought me to sit in stillness in the cool evening air and listen. Now, I'm certain God isn't directing me to throw caution to the wind. However, by leaving open space, I can hear and communicate better with Him. Even now, it also allows my spiritual cup to be filled, allowing me to be a more robust, compassionate servant mother to my adult child.

More aware of my freedom to be spontaneous with Kate, I seized many moments. When Kate was about age three, we lived in Perrysburg, Ohio. One weekday evening, I cleaned up after dinner while Kate was playing with her. On a whim, I said, "How about we go grab some ice cream?" She peered at me through curious eyes, a little confused because she was ready for bed. That didn't stop her from saying "Yay" to my idea. Then she pointed to her pajamas, and looked back at me with the same puzzled look.

"Let's go just as you are," I said. "Get your slippers."

With giggles and glee, I swept Kate into my arms and off we went. Her laughter and giddiness in the car had a way of setting my heart free. When we arrived at Churchill's, a grocery store where the staff recognized us as regulars, I put Kate in the shopping cart and headed to the ice cream aisle. Looking at Kate's face, you'd have thought she was at Disneyland. Kate chose her favorite ice cream treat and we headed to the register. She couldn't contain her excitement when she shared the ice cream adventure with the cashier. Back home we sat on the floor to enjoy the ice cream treat.

It was clear that this particular moment was not about an orange-flavored pushup but the spontaneous pajama adventure we shared. As a mom, you may do this sort of thing, too, but never think of it as merely ordinary. These moments are precious and are reinforcing your child's natural capacity for fun. These are also the moments they, and you, will remember in years to come.

From time to time, I'd suggest an impromptu change of dinner plans. I'd ask Kate if she was up for changing our dinner routine and surprise her with the idea of an indoor picnic. I'd almost always get a resounding yes. I'd hand Kate a tablecloth to spread out on the living room carpet and then she'd arrange place settings for our party of two. Kate had an extra bounce in her step as we set up our space and enjoyed our pretend *al fresco* dinner.

At least some of the time, most of us take our small kids along when we run mundane errands. These trips can also inspire impromptu games and other entertaining moments. I looked at every trip to the grocery store with Kate as an adventure or potential learning experience. This is more about attitude than anything. Change your attitude and change the experience. Naturally, she wanted to help. She also liked chatting with anyone whose attention she could grab. Sometimes, little kids are content to watch everything going on, but sometimes, they need distractions. I'd create a game or riddle to pass the time and have some fun as I loaded up our cart. As she got older and had outgrown the toddler seats, Kate would find an item on our list and then eagerly ask what was next. Little-by-little and over time she became an actual help to me.

On one shopping trip, she was ahead of me in the aisle, playfully walking backward as she repeated the item she was supposed to find. Suddenly, a scenario unfolded before my eyes and I tried to stop her from gallivanting backward toward the end of the aisle. Oops, too late! Kate backed right into an oversized display of stacked toilet paper. The tower came tumbling down on her with Kate on the floor. She was momentarily stunned and looked a little afraid as she waited for a response. Of course, we drew a small crowd of shoppers who stopped and gawked with surprise. After realizing she was alright, all I could do was laugh. That sent a message that "stuff happens" and the mishap was going to be okay. No need for fear. She laughed, too. The onlookers smiled and went on about their day. Kate exhaled and giggled as she helped me try to get the packages of toilet paper out of the way. Within seconds, we heard a voice over the loudspeaker: "Clean up in aisle ten."

Kate and I enjoyed packing the car for a last-minute trip to visit family or friends. We also took impromptu day trips or headed to an unplanned overnight adventure near our home. This often included our 125-pound golden retriever, Carson. We were always a little excited when we took off, knowing we'd be flexible about what would happen next. If you can't manage overnight excursions, then a day trip to another town or a state park is just as good.

At one time, I wouldn't have understood the fun of not knowing what was ahead. In fact, it probably would have made me nervous. As a servant mom, I also learned early on that if I didn't create these opportunities, they wouldn't happen at all. Part of leadership is *charting the course*. There were times I had to put aside my fears and all the what-ifs that came to mind. These forays into spontaneity tested my comfort level, but I took God with me when I packed the car. From a 25 mile day trip to a 700 mile drive, I made sure we had these experiences and shared these times together.

A LIFETIME OF MOMENTS

The Italian poet Cesare Pavese is well-known for saying: *We do not remember days, we remember moments.* Unconsciously, the examples I've given about spontaneity are really about moments and memories. The joy we create with our children lasts a lifetime, but the memories that form the mosaic of that joy come from moments. In the most basic way, these moments needn't cost anything. Think about creating grocery store games or spontaneous indoor picnics. You probably have moments in your past and with your kids that can serve as touchstones to remind you to create even more.

If you haven't thought about your capacity for spontaneity, do so now. Many adults have lost at least some of their capacity for spontaneity because they are focused, as I was as a young woman in college, on being responsible and setting and reaching goals. If that's happened to you, try easing back and make some space for happy surprises.

Spontaneity, like our capacity for happiness and joy, is an inside job, an internal decision. That's why we must start by considering if we've scheduled ourselves into an ever-tighter comfort zone. Of course, life isn't all or nothing. You may be a bit too rigid in one area, but flexible in another. Or perhaps you're spontaneous by nature. That's great. Keep it up. Your child is watching.

Most of us know too well how critical schedules and routines are for our kids, but we may be less aware of the value of being present with them. That's what being in the moment is all about. As I've said, I had to learn to live in the moment—it wasn't a mantra carried over from childhood. But I got it, along with embracing opportunities to connect with Kate. Believe me, Kate remembers our spontaneous moments and cherishes them.

Kids are aware of and undoubtedly comforted by predictable schedules, which give order to their lives. This is why a little spontaneity lets them know that you have the ability to create surprises and the power to change NO answers to YES, sometimes "just because." Take a look at your comfort zone and see where you need to nudge yourself out of what can seem like a safe choice but is actually a self-imposed limitation.

My journey led me to a greater understanding that our personal sense of freedom comes from within. The more we see ourselves as autonomous individuals with the ability to take charge of ourselves the more we expand our capacity to make room for moments of spontaneity in everyday life. As we embrace freedom, we create space for spontaneity to show up. And that means we're likely to see more potential for joy and laughter in our lives.

MOM MEMO
Spontaneity: An Essential Ingredient

- Create opportunities for grace-filled moments to happen by being open to them. The planned event is not always the one that makes the memory that lasts a lifetime.
- If you recognize the need to become more flexible, start by considering the gifts and possibilities spontaneity will bring your way.
- If you find yourself resisting a potential opportunity for a spontaneous change in plans, stop and consider why. Is it possible it's only a habit that's holding you back, and nothing substantial?
- Pat yourself on the back for your spontaneous moments —keep track of the moments of grace.
- Above all else, be present in the moment with your children. They watch you and remember.
- Let go, create space, and you'll see that spontaneity adds to your joy as a servant mom.

Enjoy the little things for one day you may look back and realize they were the big things.
—Robert Brault, Author

NINE

The Hug

As a Mama there will be many times in your life that you hug your child, knowing that you need that hug more than they did.

—Linda Wooten, Author

I'm a hugger. Always have been, always will be. For me, the hug is a form of communication whether I'm saying hello or goodbye or perhaps reconnecting with a friend after a long absence. A simple hug, an embrace, encapsulates and communicates our feelings in a single gesture—it speaks for itself. Although, scientific research about touch is plentiful, for the most part, it has confirmed what we already know: Touch, including hugs, is important for survival, but beyond that, for our wellbeing and growth. For a child, a hug conveys love and acceptance, and as a servant mom I can't imagine living without this exchange.

THE BENEFITS OF LOVE AND HUGS

We can list so many physical reasons why hugging is good for us. For one thing, hugging, and other kinds of touch as well, releases the oxytocin, a hormone involved in reducing stress. Almost any book written about happiness today will tell you that a hug releases dopamine and serotonin, hormones that are related to the brain chemistry of happiness. The physical and emotional effect of human touch is critical in early infant development. Being cuddled and cradled like a bug in a rug does more than soothe, protect, or delight. An infant's brain needs human warmth and contact to bond and to develop. In fact, touch is an integral part of bonding, and the overall well-being of babies and their primary caregivers.

Some of us have had to "unlearn" old school messages: *Don't pick up the baby every time she cries—that's how you'll spoil her.* Or, *if you pick up a fussy baby too much, he'll become a tyrant and won't ever leave you alone.* None of that talk sat well with me. I'm sure we wouldn't disagree that parenting is difficult and an infant who exhibits separation anxiety or fights going to bed, or cries when you place her in the car seat, or wants to be held all the time adds another dimension to feeling exhausted and being Mom. Although not a medical term, there are those babies that are defined as having high needs. They are more sensitive and easily overstimulated. Those children are often comforted by being held. For these high-needs babies, the easy wrap garments that hold the baby close to the body allow mom or dad to move about while the baby stays close and secure. It's sometimes called "baby-wearing." (Similar types of infant carrying devices are available under various names.) I regret not having one when Kate was an infant. Although she wasn't a high-needs baby, I'd have loved to "wear" my child close in a permanent hug.

Baby-wearing is not a new thing. Other cultures have traditionally wrapped their infants close to their bodies to allow mom to work while keeping their infants nearby and safe. I so enjoy seeing this swaddling and permanent hug used by today's moms and dads. It's a simple way to keep their children close while building a stronger personal bond.

No matter how you slice it, a crying baby needs cuddling and care. End of story. That's why most moms and other caregivers' first instinct is to pick up babies or toddlers in distress and hold them close. Too much love doesn't equal spoiling a child. Besides, I recall thinking that time passes quickly and it wouldn't be long before my baby girl would be leaving my arms and my lap to explore the world. Spoiling a child is a much different issue, and true, it can mix the message of servant motherhood love. That in itself has nothing to do with touch.

WE DON'T OUTGROW THE NEED

Human touch is a need that influences the structure of the brain, along with our outlook on life itself. Of course, it plays a role in how we develop both negative and positive thinking and attitudes. There are two sides of the touch coin, and, yes, we understand that touch can both soothe and frighten, but the overwhelming takeaway is that positive human touch is essential to overall wellness.

As we know, the skin is the largest organ of the body, an especially important fact I embraced throughout my professional career as a Spa Director. The spa service and treatment menu centered around the care of the skin through facials, body treatments, massage, and more. Massage has countless benefits including the power to stimulate the nervous system and reduce stress. It also includes the obvious benefits of touch. Other body treatments both exfoliate tired skin cells and stimulate new skin cells. Because the skin is receptive and responsive to touch, it brings comfort and can be an essential ingredient in the healing process. It's hard to imagine life without the sensory information we receive by way of the skin—and we can't survive without it, either.

Mothers living in a servant leadership role clearly want to comfort their child and express their love through hugging and holding. What mom isn't drawn to hold a sick child in her arms or cuddle her crying baby? For most of us, it feels automatic. And in a way it is. As a mom, touch is one of our love languages. You may be familiar with the book *The Five Love Languages* by Dr. Gary Chapman. Although addressed to couples, the information can be applied to the parent-child relationship. In love language terms, physical touch says, "I love you unconditionally." Isn't that perhaps the most important message we send? When a child is behaving the way you want her to, it's easy to hug, but as a servant mom, it's important your child feels unconditional love even in the midst of challenges and actions that you don't want to persist. Sometimes gently holding a child as you explain a corrective action or mild scolding assures them that you still love them, even as you emphasize the need for them to modify their behavior. Ending your interaction with a hug emphasizes that this is just a temporary rift.

Our children also need to feel love so they don't search for it somewhere else. The internet has its challenges with predators luring young teens toward a false sense of feeling loved and desired. Many predators are cunning and slowly manipulate young people into believing they've found a person who cares and understands them. Or there is the early boyfriend or girlfriend who temporarily fills the love bucket. Children who feel loved within their own family are less likely to (as the song goes) "look for love in all the wrong places." We as parents need to be the constant reservoir of love, no matter what the circumstance. Yes, as our children get older and gain autonomy, they need our touch less, although they'll still crave it when they're sick or hurting. They need to know that everything is going to be okay, and they will turn to you for that. Make sure your arms are open.

The language of touch changes as children grow up. Just as kids no longer crawl into a lap, a hug also might be replaced with something different, especially with boys. Maybe it's a high five or a fist bump or gentle tap on the shoulder or pat on the back. We must respect their need for space and touch them in the right way at the right time. So, while the nature of the touch may change, you can find another gesture that maintains the connection. Rest assured the hug will reappear later down the road. To this day, a hug speaks volumes about my bond with my child, a grown, mature woman.

Some children will express the need for a hug, and extending this physical affirmation is important. I did so with Kate, and now she and I easily open our arms to each other and ask for hugs. When she was still at home with me, I could be working in the kitchen or reading and Kate might walk up to me and say, "I need a hug." No explanation needed. Our hugs could be brief or measured in minutes. They could be silent or include conversation. Either way, this gesture was worth a thousand words. There were times that I made the same "I need a hug" request of Kate.

While you always want to hug your children freely, it's important to assess where they are in the moment. So, as you approach your children, make eye contact first. Read their body language. Are they in a contemplative or defensive position? Are they happily absorbed in what they're doing, or do they seem like a hug may be just what they need? If so, embrace, literally, and embrace the moment. Pay attention to the duration of the hug. No need to rush through the hug. In the "hold" position, emotions can surface and be released. Tears, tension, or sheer happiness can result, so stay right there and share the moment.

As we've probably all learned, sometimes the hard way, when someone is hurting, it's often best to say nothing. A hug can be much better than struggling to find the right words. As a servant mom, I hope my actions taught Kate that at times a hug is all that's needed. How often have we been with our child during a crisis, a disappointment, or the death of a loved one? We might anticipate what we should say or do, but we deliver the needed sentiment with a hug, a silent, firm, and physical affirmation that says, "I'm here for you."

Hugs help us detach from the stress of situations and they lighten the load. Exchanging a hug with your child can be likened to a mini-meditation or a moment of mindfulness. When crossroads and disagreements occur, share a hug. It doesn't matter if the problem or conflict persists. A hug clears the air in the moment.

A MATTER OF FAITH

From a faith perspective, I'm often reminded of the image of Jesus and the children who came to see Him. He welcomed and embraced them at times with a gentle hug. Equally important, I also learned Jesus didn't discriminate. He hugged the lepers, the outcasts and of course He hugged His mother, along with His beloved disciples. He even hugged the dirty shepherd and his sheep. Jesus's inward grace was expressed with an outward sign, a hug. It was a loving habit for Him, and I often reflected on being in the arms of Jesus. I then prayed to emulate this nondiscriminatory hug as a servant mom. I didn't need the pressure of finding the right things to say all the time. All I had to do is express my love with a simple hug.

As I reach out to love and hug my grown daughter, and others, I know I show my care in the way Jesus did. Through this fellowship and love, He lives in me and I, in turn, see Him in others. Hugging is essential to our human and spiritual growth, and it keeps me humble and grateful as a mom.

A hug is also a way to express humility. In various situations, we often struggle internally as we ask if we did the right thing. Could I have handled that better, or approached the conversation in a more effective way? My role as a servant mom taught me to embrace my mistakes and admit when I was wrong. At times I made a decision, but my reaction superseded an opportunity to pause and reflect. In other words, I reacted first and thought later. Naturally, I'd wish I could have reversed myself. I wanted a do-over. As an ever-changing servant mom, I promised myself I'd admit to being wrong and say a simple, "I'm sorry." I never heard that from my parents, so I wanted to be different for my daughter. Needless to say, I'd follow up my verbal apology with a hug, reinforcing sincerity about admitting my mistake. All along, I trusted that if my child got more hugs, she'd likely give more hugs. Now that's a wonderful thing.

MANY MESSAGES IN A SINGLE HUG

I bet you'd agree that a bear hug is the best hug of all. It needs no explanation, but it's an all-purpose, all-occasion way to say, "I missed you," or "I love you." It can communicate congratulations and is an easy way to say, "Wow, I'm so happy for you." Likewise, it also says, "I'm so sorry this happened." No words are needed. That's the hug I want to share with my child!

We can use this basic hug with others, too, as long as we know they're receptive. Some people are more reticent than others about who they invite into their arms. That's their choice, obviously, and we have no way to know the reason some people choose not to invite hugs from a particular person or on certain occasions. Cultural norms and customs also guide, or even dictate, when and who are allowed to touch. We also run into huggers who just don't know how to hug—I'm talking basic technique. Take, for instance, the side dippers, as I call them. They move in for the hug and then quickly turn their face outside the boundaries of your body, dipping significantly to one side to avoid any facial or straight-on body contact. It's pretty awkward.

Then there is the tapper hug, sometimes known as "burping the baby." They wrap their arms around you for what seems like an amazing hug to come, but when the connection is ready to be made, they lightly tap you back as if to say, "Ah, it's alright." Or, they vigorously "burp the baby." Not exactly what I'd define as a hug. We often see the "patting" hug between men. Casual and affectionate hugging between men is a relatively recent development in the U.S., although not necessarily in other parts of the world. The tapping or patting hug is a way they defuse their slight discomfort if they're not used to hugs because they didn't grow up among huggers.

The duration of a hug is important, too. The timing speaks volumes to the message encapsulated in the embrace. A casual hug is short and straightforward. But when hugging those we love or care about, a love hug calls for a more extended hold, dictated by the comfort level of the two huggers.

LEARNING EARLY

My Italian father had some strong opinions about a few things and was adamant about passing those down to his four children. Of all the tidbits he shared with us, I remember Dad's passion for the handshake and the hug. Male or female, you were to get both greetings down correctly. My dad taught us to shake hands with purpose and meaning. The handshake was to be shared with a firm grip and a meaningful shake, whether you're a man or a woman. You can probably imagine what the hug meant coming from an Italian. It had the same meaning and intent as that handshake. Whether you were family or a friend, the message was clear with one of these bear hugs. You mattered, and the communication via that hug was one of love and admiration. Even as an adult, I remember these meaningful hugs from my dad.

Tara, my Italian friend, is a loving person through and through. Her love language screams physical touch, usually by way of big hugs. I so enjoy seeing her squeeze and love on her little boy. Receiving a hug from her is like receiving a love letter. She has a message in her embrace that clearly lets you know you have been missed, are important, and matter. I remember hugging her the first time after the COVID-19 pandemic eased. The hug was strong and meaningful as if to convey all her friendship feelings in one gesture. As we embraced, we both simultaneously giggled and cried. What a message her embrace holds as the servant mother and friend she is.

LIVING WITHOUT HUGS

Unfortunately, for a variety of reasons, some people aren't huggers. But I can't imagine a life without hugs. The pandemic, especially 2020 and 2021, at its deadliest, robbed me of that love language, the ability to touch others through a hug. It was a challenge and shed light on my need for hugs, which in such a touch. We were faced with lockdowns, distancing, and quarantining that removed us not only from friends, but from family as well. The casual hug was put on hold.

I felt the lack of touch deeply, and I also observed how distancing was upsetting and confusing for so many, especially children. You may have experienced the heartbreak of telling your children they couldn't hug their grandparents. My heart was heavy when Tara described the sadness in her son's face when she had to tell Angelo they had to leave a visit with his grandparents without goodbye hugs. Three-year-olds don't understand viruses, no matter what words you try. Angelo's tears continued from the time they said goodbye to grandma and grandpa to well after their arrival home.

I've heard stories about "safe" pandemic family hugs from some inventive moms. One mom decided to hang up a piece of plastic from a clothesline. Standing on either side of the plastic, the family members embraced each other with a plastic barrier in between. Talk about recognizing the need and desire for human touch. They managed to figure out a way to hug in spite of the challenge… well sort of.

The era of COVID-19 has challenged us to alter our behavior and consider the unspoken social responses we developed when we needed to distance ourselves. Hugging is an important example. I still find myself assessing other people's body language to see if they're receptive to a hug now or still want space. Never mind our children being confused, I'm still confused.

As a result of social distancing, though, I'm more aware than ever that I'm a full-on hugger. It truly is my love language. Not that this is new, mind you. My nickname in college, given to me by one of my favorite Jesuit priests, was "The Hugger." As I walked across campus and he saw me approaching, he'd say, "Here she comes—the hugger." However, and it's important to point this out, I'm a discretionary hugger, meaning that I read others to gauge when a hug is appropriate. If it's my love language, as much as it's a part of my cultural heritage, then I also need to know when it's not welcome. If I'm unsure whether the hug will be welcome, I simply ask if hugging is okay. Or, I'll explain that I'm a hugger, just like my sweet dad-like friend Joe is. One day after Joe gave me a hug he said, "Hugging is my language. I hope that's okay with you. And if it isn't let me know."

I answered with a smile, "You're speaking my language, Joe. I'm a hugger, too, if you couldn't tell." Joe reminds me of my dad. After Dad's death in 2020, I welcome these hugs from Joe as an intercessory message from my dad. For sure, when Joe hugs someone, the other person knows there's warm intent behind the action.

My hug language continues with Kate. It was and is part of my mission as a servant mom. I've told this story before, but it's worth repeating. When Kate was little, I told her there were two things she always needed to remember about our life and my love for her. I got down on my knees to look into her eyes and hold her little hands. "Kate, remember you will *always* know you are loved, and your life will never be boring in this house. Our home will be filled with God, love, and laughter.

Once again, that was my clear mission statement. Whenever I could, a hug defined both a spoken and unspoken connection between Kate and me. After a shared belly laugh, we sealed the connection with a hug. At times of heartfelt, intimate conversations or special moments, we shared a hug. Tears, sorrow, or sickness—a hug. Hellos and goodbyes–a hug. Moments of success or moments of defeat were both marked with a hug. And just because—a hug.

Over the years, there are hundreds of pictures of Kate and me together. Looking back at them I see the familiar theme, the thread of touch and connection running through them all. The body language in the pictures is clear, and a hugging position dominates the pose in most of our images. Head in, body close, and a hug takes place. I see the hugs and feel the nonverbal message, the language of mutual respect, admiration, and love. A picture is worth a thousand words.

MOM MEMO
The Hug

- Touch your children often.
- Embrace your child when the timing is right.
- Pay attention to children's body language to help gauge what the moment calls for.
- Remember the scientific benefits of touch, including hugs, to help you manage mood and stress.
- Never underestimate the priceless power of the hug, which provides a gift to the two who share the embrace.
- Hug your child as often as you can—you'll never regret a hug

I want a hug. Not just a normal hug. One of those tight hugs that take my breath away, gives me butterflies, and makes me smile like crazy.
—Author Unknown

TEN

Cookies, Sharing, Mentoring—Servant Leaders in the Making

In the childhood memories of every good cook, there's a kitchen, a warm stove, cookies baking, and a mom.

—Barbara Costikyan, Food Writer

When I was little, my dad called me the Cookie Monster—and rightly so. Ice cream, cake, and candy as treats were okay, but for a favorite treat, nothing trumped cookies. Five nights a week, Mom, a skillful baker, packed our four lunchboxes with sandwiches and fruit, plus homemade cookies. When we were in school, Mom picked a recipe and calculated how many cookies the batch typically produced, her portion size figured at three cookies per child per lunch. Twelve cookies a day, five days a week for four kids. You do the math.

Mom was smart to bake while we were away and couldn't devour warm cookies fresh from the oven. Only rarely did we find taste testers left out on a plate when we arrived home from school. We knew the real ones were sealed in a tin and hidden from sight. And I mean hidden. Most kids wouldn't have gone through the trouble of looking for them, but I did, and I found them every time. I'd jump on a counter so I could reach the highest shelf, or maybe she'd tucked the tin inside a soup pot. I even discovered a few hiding places in the basement. No matter where Mom stashed them, I hoped to retrieve just one cookie, which meant sneaking around and concealing evidence that one might be missing. I ran the risk of messing up a potential count, but it was worth it. Although I was never confronted, I'm sure Mom knew of the infamous strikes of the Cookie Monster thief.

Not long ago, my sister Karen and I were laughing about one of our cookie escapades that happened when Mom was out. Our hurried scavenging led me to drop a can of cookies that had been hidden in a bowl on a high shelf. The cookies spilled out of the can and onto the floor, and we had bits and pieces everywhere. Frantic to cover our tracks, we returned the cookies that were still whole, and seeing no other solution, Karen and I proceeded to gobble up the evidence—every crumb and broken cookie. Then I put the cookie can back in its original hiding spot.

Mom returned home and made dinner and we gathered around the table as usual, but I was so full from eating cookies I didn't know what to do. I couldn't let on why I wasn't hungry, so I forced dinner down and held my breath until bedtime. Karen and I were sure Mom would find clues to our cookie crime. As it happened, we never heard a word about the vastly reduced number of cookies in the hidden can. I've always wondered if she knew about our prank, but decided to overlook it. Karen and I have decided to go with the notion that we got away with it, and Mom never knew the Cookie Monster struck again.

As it happens, it's possible that being a Cookie Monster is genetically passed to the next generation. I enjoyed providing homemade cookies for Kate's lunch or to share with friends when they came for a visit. When Kate was young, I knew we'd share half of most of the batches we baked. Even today, I still love baking, and it's not unusual for me to spend an evening baking cookies. Granted, this baking isn't for everyone, but whipping up a goodie from scratch relaxes me, and it gave me a way to express my creativity with new recipes or a family favorite.

Plopping the final scoop of cookie dough onto the baking sheet meant an empty bowl of cookie batter. With pre-school Kate at my side eagerly waiting for the spatula to lick or the bowl to scrape, I launched our mutual cookie-licking, batter-tasting habit.

One day, I decided to make chocolate chip cookies with my assistant Kate, about two-and-a-half at the time. As always, she stopped whatever had her attention and rushed to a kitchen chair and pushed it across the floor, which took great effort, but she didn't give up until she got it to its counter-side destination. She crawled up on the chair and assumed her ready position. We measured, we mixed, we poured, and she licked. I thought about the hygiene issues, you know, licking fingers and double dipping, and told her she couldn't lick her fingers and stick them back into the cookie dough. I had to laugh at Kate's attempt not to do this, but she kept her eyes on the prize of cleaning the mixing bowl and licking the mixing wand like it was an ice cream cone.

Sometimes, before we reached that bowl-licking stage, our final step was dumping a bag of chocolate chips into the batter—the proverbial icing on the cake for Kate. With big eyes and an eager spirit, Kate watched the mixer fold in all that chocolate goodness. On occasion I had to break the news that time was tight and that we'd bake the cookies later. Kate was less than enthusiastic about the delay, but a few chocolate chips and a thorough licking of the mixer wand satisfied her. On one particular day, I covered the bowl with plastic wrap and stored it in the refrigerator.

It was close to nap time, I asked Kate to gather a few books to read. Then I headed down the hallway to get her room ready for her nap. A few minutes later, I headed back to the playroom where I thought Kate was gathering her books, but as I passed the kitchen, I noticed the refrigerator door was wide open. There was Kate, perched on the fridge's lower register. Standing tall on her tiptoes, she was busy clawing through the cookie dough. I could only laugh! I called her name and she turned to look at me with wonderment and surprise. She was caught red-handed. There she was, a Cookie Monster in the making.

COOKIE MEMORIES

Around Christmastime, Mom baked cookies to share as gifts. Before the holiday, Mom collected empty cans of Maxwell House or Chock-Full-of Nuts aluminum coffee cans and covered the containers in festive wrapping paper—we always had a supply stored away.

Before Christmas Eve approached, Mom lined up the cans in rows on the kitchen table, which made me think of an army of tin soldiers at the ready. Mom then filled each can with a variety of homemade delicacies. Three of these, four of those, with wax paper separating the layers. I hung around hoping for a cracked or otherwise imperfect cookie, but that didn't happen often.

Mom's impressive list of cookie recipients included grandmothers, aunts and uncles, and school teachers, along with a larger box for my dad's office and a single cookie container for his boss. The mailman, the milkman, and a few neighbors were on the list as well. Then came the delivery, a job delegated to my dad and the four kids. The five of us drove off to deliver a coffee can of cookies and a Christmas wish to those on our list. We all looked forward to making our annual cookie rounds and the recipients were happy to see us coming.

When I became a mom myself, I had a new appreciation for the time it took my busy mother of four, to create, package, and share a bit of homemade goodness with so many people. I adapted this Christmas ritual to fit my circumstances and created our Christmas cookie giveaway, starting with about a dozen cookie recipes, some of which were Mom's originals, the ones I loved so much and that had earned me the Cookie Monster nickname. The process of baking and decorating creates a mess, but the music playing, flour flying, and frosting smeared on cheeks and noses made for memorable moments. Sometimes we invited friends for our cookie-decorating evenings. What fun! Every cookie was baked with joy and love. Throughout the year we surprised friends, elderly people, those unable to get out much, and anyone whose day might brighten up with homemade cookie sunshine. The tradition continues.

HANGING OUT IN THE KITCHEN

Kitchens tend to be the gathering place of choice to share a drink, lend a hand with a meal, chat about serious things, and equally important, share a laugh or two. Even if we live in a small apartment with narrow corridor style kitchen, guests and family end up hanging out wherever the table is. Maybe my half-Italian heritage is the source of my need to convene in the kitchen, but I know it's also true for people regardless of their roots. I haven't been to Italy yet, but I picture the kitchens there filled with commotion, cooking and laughter. Maybe your parents and grandparents created the same atmosphere—at least most of the time. While raising Kate, cookie baking had a special way of bringing friends and new acquaintances into our kitchen.

During Kate's childhood years, the holidays were a great time to invite friends to our home. We'd play Christmas music while we baked and frosted cookies with countless people. Our friend David was an artist and his cookie decorating skills were so exquisite we didn't want to bite into them and spoil his design. Kate and I let one of his beautiful creations harden and dry, and then we preserved it into a Christmas tree ornament and gave it to him and his partner.

There's a certain freedom to cookie decorating—no experience necessary. When we hosted novices, we pointed out a few basics and set the guests free to give it a try. Granted, most of the time, they'd end up with a dollop of frosting and a layer of sprinkles, but no one cared. Some young child was going to love that sugar-laden, frosting-covered cookie. This cookie ritual created space to welcome new acquaintances to our home, a frequent occurrence because we moved around a lot and had to start over in each locale.

Growing up, the kitchen was my mom's domain. She was a great cook, and in order to get the job done, her space was off-limits. Sure, I dried dishes and washed and chopped vegetables, but that was about it. Regardless of copious cookies in our house, I learned the basics of baking—and cooking—in my favorite home economics class in middle school, not at home. Later, when I was married, I figured cooking out on my own, following recipes and experimenting, although the first meal I made as a married woman came from a box of Hamburger Helper. When I served it for dinner, my husband politely asked, "Did you drain the grease off the hamburger?"

Oh my. "Really? Was I supposed to?"

We laughed and realized that I had so much to learn.

Cookie-Cutter Cookies

These tasty cookies are our go-to-recipe when it's time to make cut-out cookies. Their shortbread taste makes them a family favorite. Making them ahead of time, cutting them out and freezing until ready to decorate preserves their yummy taste and texture.

Cooking with love

FROM THE KITCHEN OF Marie & Kate

Cookie-Cutter Cookies

1 cup (2 sticks) butter at room temp — 1/2 cup sugar
2 & 1/2 cups flour — 1 tsp almond / lemon extract

Cream together butter and sugar. Blend in flour. Mix well and pat dough into a ball. Refrigerate for 2 hours. When ready to make cookies heat the oven to 300 degrees. Roll cookies on floured board to about 1/4 inch thickness. Cut shapes with cookie cutters. Place on an ungreased cookie sheet. Bake for 20 to 25 minutes until lightly brown around the edges. Cool for 15 minutes. Decorate with frosting as desired.

SHARING SPACE AND TIME

I recommend that parents share their cooking space with their kids. As the kids get older, give them a recipe and instructions for their favorite dishes and let them have at it. Many a good adult cook started by fixing parts of meals for the family—especially important when parents are working long hours and the kids are expected to help.

Maybe cooking isn't a big deal in your family, but perhaps your garden shed or workshop defines what's important to you. Let the kids watch you at work and ask questions. They'll likely also ask to try some projects. Great. Provide clear instructions, supervise when necessary, and then relinquish control. Other than some basic guidelines, and safety rules, we need to let go of the premise that to be done correctly something always has to be done our way. Oh, how difficult it often is to get out of our own way.

Creating food from a recipe is a time to share what you know about measuring ingredients, following instructions, and taste-testing the final product. By learning with and from you, your kids will accept that mistakes happen and recipes can flop—sometimes in spectacular fashion. But they also have the incomparable pleasure of great success when the outcomes exceed expectations.

The same is true for growing roses or tomatoes, or fixing a lamp or building a bookcase. Success or mishap, your children will see beauty in the outcome when you handle the entire process with grace, patience, and humility. That lesson lasts for a lifetime. (Some of these escapades make for the best family stories, too.)

When Kate finished graduate school she moved into a small apartment in Rhode Island. Baking Christmas cookies wasn't going to be easy in her small space, but it didn't matter. It was going to happen. She wanted to host the cookie baking at her place and I was all in. I packed up the goods and headed north.

Our family's Italian cookie was on our list of must have choices. We'd made the recipe before so we weren't novices. We made the batter and baked the first batch. When we pulled the sheet out of the oven, Kate and I looked at each other in dismay. Something went wrong. We tasted them and laughed. Oops. Somehow, somewhere, the recipe was altered. Time to start over. The cookies and the remaining batter were destined for the garbage.

Our failed attempt wasn't much different from other life experiences gone awry, and as most of us do, day in and day out, we cut our losses in time and money and kept going. Italian cookies didn't make it into the Christmas giveaways that year, but we shrugged it off and said, "There's always next year."

FIND YOUR "THING"

If you can manage it, find something that involves preparing food to share with your child—and it can be something both parents do. Maybe Dad is the pasta maker and Mom is the baker. It doesn't matter if you're good at it when you start. Start with pre-made cookie or pizza dough, especially if you find yourself overwhelmed, but you still want to share jointly prepared food with your children. But if you can, try following a recipe from scratch at least once—kids love measuring and pouring ingredients and finding just the right utensil in the drawer.

For many kids, the best part of the process and the memory is sharing. Look at me. I'm still talking about driving around in the car with my siblings and dad to deliver our cans of cookies. The real payoff is not only in the product but in the joy of giving it away to neighbors or other relatives or people in need. Many churches ask adults to bring food to a bereaved family or one overwhelmed by an illness. If you bring a casserole or a fresh loaf of bread or a tin of cookies, if it's appropriate to the situation, let your children come with you when you deliver it. Although not literally a "random act of kindness," as the phrase goes, this kind of sharing is an integral part of mentoring your child.

If your thing is gardening, that can be much like baking in terms of learning and then sharing the fruits of your labors. Let your children see you take flowers to a neighbor or deliver fresh produce to the food pantry or homeless shelter. Equally important, point out other people who do these things, so your kids absorb how many different ways exist to show servant leadership.

Let them be part of packing up books and toys and clothes they've outgrown. If you can, take them with you when you donate the items to the resale shop or charity sale. If your service involves your time, rather than a product, make sure your children understand what you're doing and why.

As servant moms, sharing time and opportunities with our children is one way we help them develop into servant leaders. However, in order to become leaders, children must first learn to listen to God. Like many adults, they're often so busy petitioning, asking for this or that, doing the talking and the directing, that they forget to stop and listen. It's up to us to remind them that God wants us to hear from Him. It's in the silence, the quiet space in our heart that He speaks. By learning to listen, children first become good followers, which then develops the capacity to be strong leaders, regardless of personality traits. Teaching our kids to listen, focus, follow, and execute instructions whether from a coach or a boss, or from a parent in the kitchen, provides the groundwork, the foundational piece for our children to develop into strong servant leaders.

Leadership is influence, walking the talk and being "the light of the world" for all to see. Embrace the fact that you are creating time and significance around a small gesture of teaching, creating, and sharing. Let your children know how important their efforts are. Reinforce that with assurances that they are leading and are becoming the salt and light as Jesus commanded. These childhood actions, delivering baked cookies or carrots from their family garden is the beginning of obeying God's call to leadership.

Today, I see that Kate has become a servant leader. She cares about the wellbeing of others, but doesn't neglect her own need to grow and raise her effectiveness in this world. So, did this start with our cookie journey? I believe that journey revealed more than I ever could have imagined. Our cookie baking went beyond celebrating the holidays or having a treat. It was a mentoring event, which later became the backdrop for communication and laughter fests, not to mention a venue for creativity.

Kate and I baked for birthdays, weddings, picnics, and just because people awaited our homemade cookie goodness. Delectable cookies became our signature gift, our thing. Our cookie jar was full just in case friends stopped by or we needed to mail a care package to a college dorm. Even today, if company is coming and the cookie jar is near empty, I often whip up a quick batch. I always keep baking supplies around.

Some rituals stick, and although family and work schedules dictate our availability, we set a date for our annual Christmas cookie-bake. We make a list, check it twice, and we still deliver cookies to friends and family. Kate and I share a mission to "pay it forward," and baking and sharing is a way to do that while we also enjoy our companionship. More memories are waiting in the wings and in our kitchens.

As time passes, you will recognize the gift of this type of quality time shared with your children. If you stay in the moment, you may be surprised by the thoughts your child, young or older, share or the creativity that comes through. For many of us, the kitchen is where the magic happens. Let it be a place to gather in your home, and you'll find it a place where precious memories are created. There's always the possibility that you have a Cookie Monster of your own waiting in the wings.

MOM MEMO
Cookies, Sharing, Mentoring—
Servant Leaders in the Making

- Find your special "thing" that's a source of fun, companionship, and sharing. A signature cookie, dish, or family recipe can become part of a ritual that your children always remember and associate with the gift of sharing.
- Regardless of how much or how little shared baking or cooking takes place, make your kitchen a welcome place to gather and where lines of communication are always open.
- Never negate the thoughtfulness of bringing homemade meals, bread, or cookies from your kitchen to others. Keep the gesture alive, and perhaps your children will pick it up, too.
- In small gestures of teaching, creating, and sharing you're mentoring your children, preparing them for servant leadership.
- If food rituals aren't for you, find your own way to create special sharing moments with your children and others. From gardening to costume-making to being a reliable volunteer, as a servant mom you have unique ways to share your spirit with your kids and others.

ELEVEN

ROUTEEN—Speak Their Language

Teach your daughter to worry less about fitting into the glass slippers and more about shattering the glass ceilings.

—Melissa Marchonna, Digital Marketer, NY Jets

The tagline, "So Routine, So Not," was positioned below the logo of "ROUTEEN," a trademarked, performance-based group for teenagers I created while living in Petoskey, Michigan. The program was designed to share the message of confidence, healthy living, and positive self-esteem through music, dance, and short skits. Experienced and non-experienced dancers were invited to participate, based on the simple theme: You are welcomed here!" The point of the program was to get kids moving.

ROUTEEN came to fruition shortly after Kate and I relocated to Northern Michigan, where I'd accepted my new position as Spa Director for a destination ski company. Moving meant saying goodbye to friends and family, clubs and activities. While going through the inevitable sense of loss, this new chapter opened up fresh opportunities and adventures. For Kate, leaving her dance school was a significant loss, because she'd enjoyed the classes and the challenging work of dance, along with the friendships she'd formed.

Kate was adamant about continuing dance lessons in our new locale, and I was happy to agree. Dance brought her joy, but it also developed self-discipline and nurtured poise and self-confidence. Being a dancer myself I looked back on the lasting lessons I'd learned, so I was personally very happy that she loved it so much. We began a search for a dance studio in our new hometown, but found minimal opportunities. After a few attempts and several strikeouts I was at a loss about where to turn next.

In addition to my full-time job, I also taught group fitness classes at a downtown fitness center. As it happened, the second-floor studio had beautiful hardwood floors and full-length mirrors, a perfect space for both dance and fitness classes. One day I had the idea of starting classes for tweens and teens because this age group is often overlooked and under-served when it comes to fitness, and a gap certainly existed in our area. It came as no surprise that Michigan ranked as one of the top ten worst states in the country for childhood obesity. It seemed like a place ripe for a fitness mission. And so ROUTEEN began to take shape.

ROUTEEN evolved into an afterschool program, involving middle school and high school students in physical movement and performance productions that would motivate and deliver a positive message to the participants and audiences of all ages. I found a way to incorporate and showcase whatever unique talents each child revealed. What had been hidden were the teens' gifts for movement and showmanship, and the camaraderie they developed along the way improved not only their lives but the lives of others.

Part of my premise for ROUTEEN was that most kids love some type of music, and for some, love of music invites the desire to dance. As I worked with more and more kids, finding their comfort level came naturally to me. Once I saw who and what I had to work with, I could choreograph accordingly. I welcomed their input, and many suggested dance steps themselves. The more contributions they made, the more investment they had in the project. I was all about inclusion, so this was perfect! I was also amazed by their ease and speed in memorizing choreography. Ah! The power of a young mind. I often told the group to remember the routine after our practice because I would most likely forget it, even though I choreographed it. They came through without fail when my mind drew a blank on what came next.

The teens produced a major production each spring, and they also participated in parades and formed a traveling performance group. ROUTEEN provided halftime shows at local sports events, and enjoyed a visit to the governor's mansion. The concept behind ROUTEEN even made it to Las Vegas, where as it happened, a group of kids from the inner city Boys & Girls club of Las Vegas, performed as the opening act for the International Spa Association's Annual Conference, at The Venetian Resort Hotel.

Since I had been involved in the spa industry for over 10 years and was a member of the International Spa Association (ISPA), I had an idea. By 2002, the industry was awakening to the health and wellness needs of young adults as an emerging market. With that population–in mind, I submitted a proposal to the event committee suggesting that a group of kids could be the opening act at the conference.

I had a desire to provide local Las Vegas inner-city kids a unique opportunity to perform, which was the reason behind my proposal. I believe that being on stage, even once, can be life changing. I've witnessed this kind of transformation many times as a teacher, a director, and choreographer. I believe the reward of performing and saying "I did it," resonated inside each performer, not to mention receiving positive feedback from the sound of the audience's roaring applause rewarding their hard work.

THE VISION BECOMES REALITY

First, I had to initiate the process to make my vision a reality. Coincidentally, my spa supervisor had lived in Vegas. She contacted her dad, and he suggested I contact Ginger, the Director of the local Las Vegas Boys & Girls Club. After explaining the opportunity to perform at the upcoming conference, she agreed to help and soon became as excited as I was about the challenge ahead. We gathered a group of roughly twenty teenagers. Then, I developed and submitted my official proposal to the International Spa Association, asking them to sponsor the endeavor, which would involve underwriting my travel expenses to Las Vegas to direct the group of teens. It meant choreographing the performance and holding two back-to-back all day rehearsals. We'd have less than thirty hours to teach choreography and perfect the routine for the opening performance for a conference crowd of over 5000. Challenging, yes, but I was completely confident this could be done. Apparently, the conference planners were, too, because they accepted the proposal. *Viva Las Vegas!*

With the association's funding in place, I was in high gear, arranging music and choreography these honorary ROUTEEN members would perform. I also was well aware I would be "parenting" children at an impressionable age for a short but significant event in their lives.

I relied on Ginger, an energetic and positive force, to provide brief background information on each of the young people in the group, the majority of whom were raised in single parent households and were among Las Vegas' most economically disadvantaged. Like Boys & Girls Clubs everywhere, this one served as a safe haven after school and on weekends and it was a place to hang out during the summer. I prayed for the gift to empower these kids and ignite even a small nudge of confidence in their future, through the power of performing, even if it was just once. The benefits of teamwork and following directions, along with inclusion and mutual respect, were among the other experiences I believed the teens would gain. These were the same qualities ROUTEEN provided my students in Michigan.

It is important to mention that I was still a single mom, working full time for Boyne USA as Director of the Spa and doing ROUTEEN in the evenings with occasional weekend practices. Now I added this Vegas event on top of it. Of course the activities I created meant Kate was involved so how perfect was that? She loved our Michigan group, and she recruited her friends, both male and female. Sometimes I look back at the energy I had and I can't believe I did all of this. But it never felt like work. Crazy!

I scheduled two weekend trips to Las Vegas, the first to introduce and clarify our mission and tackle at least half of the choreographed conference piece the kids would be performing. It was a fast-tracked lesson on trust and acceptance, as in trusting the good intentions of this mission, trusting me as the teacher, and trusting each other. Finally, a nonnegotiable principle was the acceptance of each other and embracing the abilities of each person's skill level. It was a bit of a tough sell, but the group of now sixteen teens agreed to the terms.

Although I had choreographed the entire piece, flexibility was the name of the game. After assessing the talent that showed up, I would then adjust the choreography to match the skill levels within the group. The enthusiasm coupled with the desire to dance provided the foundation for a strong group, with some work needed on attention span and self-discipline. But it all came with the territory. All in all they were a great group of kids.

This first weekend broke the ice and nurtured trust between the teens and me. I also learned more about each one of the kids and their current situations. Single-parent households, often because of divorce, had disrupted family life, and in some cases, abuse and chaos characterized their home life. Some kids had an incarcerated parent, and in many cases, these teens were forced to operate independently without much of a safety net. However, joy began to emerge as the kids engaged in self-expression through this dance journey. After weekend one, I flew home believing the impact on the teens was even more powerful than I'd expected. Between the first weekend and my next trip back two weeks later, I hoped they'd remember the routine. Even more important, I asked myself if they'd come back for round two. Only time would tell.

I wished I could share the weekend experience with Kate and the local ROUTEEN members, but I couldn't take them with me and had to settle for knowing they'd be there in spirit. Somewhere in my mind I was conjuring up a way to at least take Kate with me, to have her see the performance and have a getaway experience with mom. I was going to work on that.

FROM KINDNESS TO ACCEPTANCE

Accepting others for who and what they are was a mantra in our house. When Kate shared a criticism of someone from school or volleyball practice or the choir, I'd gently and softly say, "Don't judge." An underlying theme I stressed to Kate, along with reminding myself, is that we are here to accept others and live with kindness. It's not our role to judge others. So often we don't know the back story of a child, their family or their current situation. How can we? So how do we have the right to assume or judge others, their looks, their actions, or even their silence?

Teaching young children about acceptance starts by teaching kindness, which is about being aware and acting from the heart. It's a message I taught Kate at a young age, taken from my faith-filled background based on the universal message of: *Do unto others as you would have done unto you.* Whether a child is hard-wired with empathy at birth is another discussion, but I do believe many are born with the gene that gives them the ability to intuitively understand others by emotionally entering their world. It seems to come easily and develop naturally if you start early talking to your children about understanding how others may feel. Compassion begins with empathy.

Kindness can be expressed in words and actions. Doing so creates confidence, bestowing self-worth on another and sends the message that says, "I care." In a sense it helps create the foundation for acceptance. Acts of kindness can go far to exemplify an attitude that conveys the message, "I care." Small kind gestures can make someone's day, change the course of tough times, and send a message of hope. It demonstrates inclusivity and says in its own way, "All are welcome here." Holding a door, bringing an extra snack to share, or saying hi to a new student can change the course of another person's day. Saying thank you or "great job" to a child are words that exemplify more than the obvious.

As parents, we need to model kindness for our children. Watch what happens with your child as they mimic your thoughtfulness and heartfelt compassion. In the big picture of life, kindness brings peace. And isn't that what we want for our children and for the world they will live in? Simple gestures, meaningful words, big rewards?

When I'd come home after the first weekend, Kate was eager to hear about the group and the outcome of the two-day practices. After talking about the life circumstances around some of the teens, Kate quickly realized this group was different from the local ROUTEEN in Petoskey. My heart was heavy as I described the unpredictable situations and daily challenges these kids faced. I attempted to re-create the practice sessions for Kate, both the outbursts, the unruliness at times, but also the laughter. Bottom line, the group embraced the music, the moves, and the whole concept of performing. Kate knew about the joy of performing, the teamwork, and the feeling of satisfaction when she worked and prepared for a performance.

This back-and-forth conversation with Kate was invigorating, eventually leading me to blurt, "Would you like to come and be a part of this production?" I'd wanted Kate to be a part of this experience from the very beginning but the logistics were complicated. Without delay though, Kate was enthusiastic about coming along.

I had a bit of homework to do in presenting this offer to Ginger and the Las Vegas group. Questioning my eagerness as mom, I second-guessed my spontaneous offer. But not for long. It was too late to back out. I'd invited Kate, the same as a promise, and even though she was only twelve at the time, I'd make it work. I needed to present my idea to involve Kate to the existing Boys & Girls Club group. It was a courtesy to ask them, versus telling them I'd made a decision. Although all ethnic backgrounds, ages, and walks of life were represented in this Las Vegas group, some lifestyles and opportunities were different from Kate's. Besides, I was asking this group with whom I'd built a relationship to add age diversity by accepting a 12-year-old girl into their world, sight unseen. It also meant welcoming yet another person from outside their Las Vegas community.

Along with those factors, Kate would need to learn the nuts and bolts of the performance number at home, since she couldn't come along on the second weekend trip out to Vegas for practice. She'd practice with the group only on the day of the event. However, Kate has a fabulous memory for dance to match her love for it, so I was confident she'd be fine. More important, her tender heart and silent leadership would make her a shoo-in with the Vegas group.

Two weeks passed quickly, and arriving back at the Boys & Girls Club was like coming home again. The crew was excited about my return and ready to practice. Honestly, I'd held my breath on the flight, wondering if the commitment to performing had stuck with these young adults. I had no guarantee they'd return to the second practice. Their commitment was their word, and frankly I was praying that was enough. With ROUTEEN as the opening act for the conference, there was no turning back now.

The young people all showed up and were waiting for me in the lobby—enthusiasm ran high. When we arrived at the gym to practice and the group took their spots, I was distracted by a hole in the formation. Someone was missing. "Where is Tanisha?" I asked.

One of the other young men piped up. "Oh, she's not gonna be here. She stole a car. She's gone."

Well, that's a valid reason to not show up. My heart was heavy with sadness for some of the life choices these kids were confronted with every day. I said a prayer for Tanisha and asked God to protect her. I also asked that this performance influence these kids, even just one, in a positive way. I also adjusted and reviewed the choreography and the dancers' attitudes before launching our practice. Enthusiasm to move took over and their memories served them well. This routine was shaping up. Talent was on display and a sense of pride emerged, as if to say, "I got this."

When lunchtime rolled around, I brought up the topic of adding one more person to the group and mentioned Kate. After a few questions and a sense of protection around their current project, they agreed to welcome Kate to fill the hole left by Tanisha's absence. Of course, I was thrilled. In my heart, I knew this would provide an underlying lesson for the group, for Kate, and for me.

The weekend's final practice was stellar. We were all excited with the results of this somewhat complicated routine. With only four days of practice time, the team had mastered the steps, along with developing trust and teamwork.

The proof was in the pudding. Showtime was only two weeks away and we had prep work to do. We discussed logistics of performance day, including finalizing the wardrobe, makeup, and more. Industry vendors donated T-shirts to go along with the dancers' choice of either comfy jeans or shorts. Given this was a spa industry event, two of my colleagues who owned a skincare company offered makeup services.

Two weeks flew by. As I watched Kate practicing at home to perfect the routine on her own, my pre-performance energy and enthusiasm intensified. The professional soundtrack I'd had made permeated the house every single day. I thought of the lessons and opportunities already achieved from preparing for this twelve-minute performance. (If you know anything about dance, you know twelve minutes is a long time.) I also reflected on my experiences to that point. In the relatively short time I'd spent with the Las Vegas kids, a special bond had formed. Time had been short, so productivity was vital. At times I'd pushed, demanded respect, and accentuated precision, while all along, walking a fine line of tough love and encouragement. As in any group of teens, a few had enough confidence and attitude to make up for those who didn't. Either way, it was amazing to see firsthand how their self-confidence surfaced. No wonder the experience had already inspired hope in my heart.

Arriving at The Venetian Resort Hotel with a middle schooler was a lot like entering the sensory overload of Disneyland. There was so much to see. When we headed to see the stage and setup for the opening of the conference, I was taken aback with my first glimpse of our venue. At the time, this 50,000 square foot, four-tier nightclub was regarded as the largest, most decadent night club in Las Vegas. These kids were not performing in a ballroom. They were performing on a nightclub stage that showcased some of the greatest Vegas performers. Wow... even I was a bit intimidated.

The Boys & Girls Club had arranged transportation for all the teens. The van arrived, and so did an enthusiastic yet nervous bunch of teens. Their energy exploded when they saw the nightclub stage from which they would be performing. Our rehearsal time was to start soon. Music was given to the audio techs and lighting was devised to mirror this energetic montage of music.

As the group was about to take the stage for practice, one of the participants, Jackie, came to me and said, "I'm not doing this."

"What?" This was a sudden turnaround.

"It's stupid. I'm not doing this." Using a bit of coaching and motherly support, I attempted to ask why and acknowledge all the hard work she had already put forth for this performance. With a show of attitude, she repeated, "I'm not doing this," and stormed off. I followed her in hopes of getting to the real reason behind her abrupt decision. As I called her name, she stopped and turned around. The uncompromising attitude she had displayed all along finally prevailed in what was now her reason to quit. I played all the cards I knew to convince her to perform: her talent, time invested thus far, teamwork, and more. Jackie didn't bite. She was petrified to get on stage. No coercing or pushing would change her mind. I left the conversation by letting her know she'd be missed.

I shared the news with the group that we were down one performer and watched the panic displayed on the faces in front of me. Confidence and commitment were the keys to performing, I explained to the group. "Things happen. And as they say, the show must go on." The team nodded their heads enthusiastically. "We got this," they said, nearly in unison. And the truth is they did.

With the clock ticking, I had little time to waste. But first, I introduced Kate to the group. She met the teens she didn't know and would be performing with for the first time. Kate's terrific dance memory eliminated the choreography issue, but she faced the uncertainty about being included and accepted. That's all I prayed for, acceptance, for my child and the group.

Hellos were exchanged, and even the older kids accepted the much younger member of the group and pulled Kate right in. She also dealt with the task at hand, making quick friends and mastering the routine. The practice was a success, especially considering we had to adjust for Jackie's walk-away. ROUTEEN T-shirts were handed out, makeup was completed. It was showtime.

The excited kids waited anxiously in the wings for their cue to begin. I headed center stage first to deliver my introduction, emphasizing the need of the Spa Industry to attend to an emerging market in wellness—our young adults. I described how this group came together, their commitment, and how in just four days they'd worked together to perfect this routine.

The crowd roared. The energy was contagious. My heart swelled with pride for how far they'd come, for the opportunity they were offered, and their willingness to show up as they were, Kate included. Now they'd been given an enthusiastic audience. I could feel it.

Suddenly, the lights went down, music started, and the song "Let's Get Loud" filled the space. A rush of enthusiasm penetrated the room as ROUTEEN took over the stage. Within minutes the entire audience was up, dancing and moving with the music. The routine was executed perfectly with dance, gymnastics, ribbons rippling in color, and rhythm moves to fill the stage. Camaraderie and teamwork prevailed. On their feet, the audience cheered for these novice dancers.

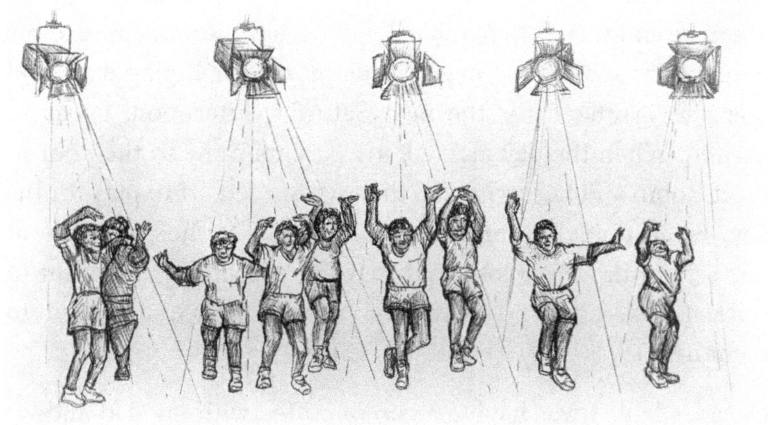

It was hard to miss the smiles on the kids' faces, including my daughter's. She did a fantastic job, but more important, she merged with an unknown group of kids and was part of creating an exquisite experience for everyone involved. The memory of their smiling young faces and our group hug after the performance will remain with me forever. I was the proud one, both of this effort, and their accomplishment. But just as special was the fact that Kate was with me to experience and embrace this life changing opportunity.

This ROUTEEN performance showed Kate, once again, the value of diversity and inclusion. Diversity means different. It is accepting others for who they are. Inclusion is about empowerment of all people and creates a sense of belonging. This group of inner city kids in Las Vegas demonstrated the importance of respecting others and providing all with the same opportunities, regardless of their circumstances. This particular opportunity demonstrated in real time what inclusion is all about. This lesson in diversity celebrated how we might all have differences but more importantly how we are alike.

Years ago I shared a story with Kate that involved my best friend Robin. Robin and I went to Catholic grade school together and were inseparable. Eager to have Robin come to my house after school, we begged our moms for a play date, and one was arranged for the next Saturday afternoon. I was so excited. When the day arrived, my parents came to the door to meet Robin and her mom and then we headed off to play for the day. From that time on our friendship flourished throughout our school days. We lost contact when we both moved out of state. (Now, after 30 years Robin and I have managed to reconnect.)

Decades later I was having a cup of coffee with my dad and we were talking over various ideas, including acceptance and differences, certainly topics of our time. My dad then said, "You know Marie, years ago when you invited Robin over to our home for the first time, you never mentioned to your mother and me that she was black."

Hmm… I thought. I probably didn't think about it because it didn't matter to me. It didn't matter then, nor does it today. Robin was my friend, so nothing else was important. At the time, Robin being black was noteworthy to my parents and to their generation, but decades later, for many, it would be of no particular note.

THE WORLD BEYOND THE FRONT DOOR

We'd have a different world if young people were guided to take a few steps beyond the world around them into unfamiliar territory, which then pushes them, with the support of adults, beyond their familiar social boundaries and home court advantage. Let's call these experiences a move out of the "comfort zone." A comfort zone is a psychological state of familiarity, ease, and comfort. Or we could say it's familiar energy. If we let it, it can have a mind of its own, which might lead us away from our greatest aspirations. It can stop us dead in our tracks. Not only that, our comfort zone provides us with excuses about why we cannot move forward or try something different. It often uses fear as its greatest tool to keep us stuck.

Kids have comfort zones and have their way of finding them. Pay attention to how and what creates discomfort or avoidance and you'll see a potential "comfort zone." Kate might have said, "I don't want to dance with older kids I don't know." Period, end of story. What if she had misinterpreted the buzz of nervous energy at the prospect of participating and thought that energy was bad—a warning? Like fear. Think what she would have missed. The same goes for the group of teens I worked with in Las Vegas. Nervousness and excitement can feel similar. Like Jackie, apprehension might tell us to misread our environment and acting out of fear, say no.

Think of all the things we might have missed (or are missing right now) because we were afraid to say yes to something (potentially beneficial, fun, adventurous) that was luring us out of our comfort zone. I'm not talking about extreme risk or dangerous undertakings or any such thing.

I know God calls us out of our comfort zone. He wants us to live our dreams, to share our gifts, but to embrace possibilities we need to accept that the comfort zone is constantly challenged. It is never idle. Nor is God. Listening and paying attention to when we feel an urge, or what I like to call a nudge, means complacency is being challenged. Opportunities or ideas present themselves, and a variety of feelings and self-talk begin. Stepping into a new situation involves some challenge, not one that challenges safety or good judgment, yet one that would be worth embracing.

Taking change and new opportunities for prayer mean we are involving God in the nudge He has initiated. Through wisdom and prayer, we step out of our comfort zone and trust God. When we pray and listen, God will lead us to the right decision. As I think back, I was challenged often to step out of my comfort zone for the good of both Kate and me. As soon as I thought we were settled in a new place, I felt a tap on my shoulder, as if God was saying, "Well done here my disciple. I have another place for you to be. Time to move on."

These new moves, opportunities, and personal chapters pushed not only me, but Kate, too, far out of our comfort zones. The risk appeared to be worth the reward, and that is when I knew God was present in my stepping out. Of course, there were ups and downs associated with each new adventure, but looking back I'm grateful for the push out of my comfort zone. Personal growth, revelations, and lessons learned have been life-changing.

THE PREP WORK

It's important not to force or push our children's boundaries or our own without first conducting an assessment of the situation. A parent who lacked childhood opportunities might push her children into all kinds of activities and lessons because she wants them to have what she missed. The term "over-scheduled child" resulted from this frenzy for childhood "experiences."

On the other hand, sometimes we hold children back by imposing our comfort zone on them. The fact is, as your children grow up and are in school and participate in various activities, they'll encounter many situations unfamiliar to you, but which may become part of their comfort zone.

Exposing your child to a new situation or opportunity, one slightly out of their normal routine, can influence their outlook on life in countless ways and may have an impact on the lives of others too. Create an activity or an event that takes your child away from their surroundings and to places where they may see other cultures and the way others live, maybe in your city or town. Give your child the ability to experience and learn from another group of children. Kids need exposure to more so that they can learn the many lessons that life is waiting to teach them—right outside their normal routines.

ROUTEEN™

MOM MEMO
ROUTEEN—Speak Their Language

- Within a controlled environment, nudge your kids out of their comfort zone.
- Demonstrate kindness to others with words and simple acts of kindness.
- Teach your child the importance of simple gestures: establish social greetings, such as saying hello and

asking after the other person, holding a door, paying a compliment, and learning how to play "nice."

- Remember to be kind to your kids first. This nurtures mutual respect. It sounds simple, but at times we forget the simplest acts or words are what provide a consistent underlying message of love.
- Explore opportunities outside of your everyday routine to enrich your children's lives.
- Help your kids understand that feeling a little nervous about a new pursuit is okay. They can take on a challenge outside their comfort zone with greater enthusiasm when they recognize the difference between nervous excitement and actual danger.
- Life is bigger than where we live. Get involved in a service project, sponsor a child through a reputable faith-based organization, or even create a project of your own with your child, your family, or your community. Life lessons will happen and a lasting impact will be made.

And as we let our own light shine, we unconsciously give other people permission to do the same.
—Marianne Williamson, Author, Spiritual Advisor

TWELVE

In Search of the Right Thing—Saying Goodbye

When life is sweet say thank you and celebrate. And when life is bitter say thank you and grow.

—Shauna Niequist, Author and Christian Leader

To state the obvious, divorce is never easy. If you've been through it or are in the midst of a divorce now, then you know it brings with it not only inevitable changes, but upheavals that wear on the heart and soul.

Selling the family home is one of those emotion-laden challenges. With my divorce in process, we had to put our house up for sale, which meant we had to spend extra time keeping the house presentable for showings. Meanwhile, I also looked for a rental option for Kate, our pup Samantha, and me. Renting an apartment or house is challenging enough, but finding a place that accepted pets added one more obstacle to overcome. With fervent prayer and belief, I prayed that God would provide and I would find a house, preferably, near our neighborhood so I could keep Kate in familiar surroundings and close to her playmates.

It wasn't long before a pet-friendly, three-bedroom ranch with a beautiful yard and finished basement became available right in our neighborhood. Kate, Sam, and I immediately made this new space our home. It's a cliché, but it's true: *Home is where the heart is.*

Some goodbyes are much harder than others. But, given the circumstances, it wasn't difficult for me to leave my former house and claim a new life, complete with a new environment.

One day after work, I put the leash on Sam and we ventured out on our afternoon walk, always Sam's favorite part of the day. However, my usually energetic, people-pleasing golden retriever seemed sluggish. This was highly unusual. "Come on, Sam." I gently tugged on the leash. Her less-than-aggressive response indicated something was off. I reversed course and headed back home, but because of Sam's behavior that day, it was a slow, meandering walk. Once inside, Sam immediately searched for a place to rest.

Over the next few days, Samantha became more lethargic. She also had no appetite, refusing even her favorite treats. It was time to call the vet. After an anxious description of her symptoms, the vet offered an appointment later that same day. I left the vet's office that day without answers, but Sam's blood and other specimens were sent out for testing.

A few days later, the vet called with the news I'd dreaded. Seven-year-old Sam had cancer. Worse, treatment options were few and far between. A cancer treatment facility was about three hours away, but the cost was exorbitant, and of course, there was no guarantee of success. Stunned by the news, I struggled as I considered my next steps. Difficult questions rapidly filled my mom brain. How would I break the news to four-year-old Kate? How would I find the right words? When is the best time to tell her? How do I explain the death of a pet? How will she respond? As young as she was, Kate knew Sam wasn't feeling well.

Samantha had been my faithful companion during my pregnancy, especially since my husband was away at sea for most of the time. The day I brought newborn Kate home, the friendly retriever was the first to welcome her. Sam was a constant in Kate's life, a reliable buddy, but now her buddy was struggling. Because of the ultimate outcome, I was in turmoil over the conversation I needed to have with Kate.

Trusting that my heart would lead me to find the right way to share with Kate the heart-wrenching news about Sam, I found a moment that felt right and chose the age appropriate words that would help her understand the situation.

As any mom—or dad—knows we not only intellectually understand our children's pain, but we actually feel it right along with them. This is part of the mystery of the parent-child bond. We long to take away the specific cause of their discomfort, the impending or actual loss and the pain that goes with it. But our intellectual self soon brings us to the realization that some things can't be fixed. Some situations need to be faced head-on.

This situation put my servant motherhood skills to the test, and helped me strengthen them, too. I needed to comfort and empathize while encouraging Kate to express her own feelings as they came up. One evening after dinner, I explained that Sam was sick. I was honest with Kate explaining that the dog had little time left with us. Disbelief was followed by tears. Our joint grief was compounded by the fact that time was running out.

We cried together that evening as we talked about our memories of Sam while sharing hugs between stretches of contemplative silence. We faced a bumpy ride. Kate hurt. I hurt… I hurt for Sam herself, and I hurt for Kate. Holding Kate tight was all that made sense at that moment.

Moving forward, the primary goal was to make our dear Sam as comfortable as possible. The vet urged us to enjoy our time with her. “Go ahead and feed her whatever she wants,” he advised.

We took great pleasure sharing every Popsicle, ice cream cone, and snack with Sam. "One for me and one for Sam, please," Kate would say. Then Kate and Sam would sit comfortably on the back porch enjoying their special treats. That vivid memory still lingers—and always will. Kate loved her furry buddy and her furry buddy loved her back.

A couple of weeks passed. Sam’s downward spiral was painful to witness. One night Sam was in her familiar spot on the floor next to my bed. In the dark the sound of labored breathing roused me out of what was already restless sleep. I lay still, carefully listening, with tears rolling down my cheeks. Sam was fighting to breathe. The medication was no longer enough to keep her comfortable. Her quality of life had rapidly deteriorated. This situation couldn't continue any longer. It was selfish of me to keep Sam alive simply because we couldn’t bear to be without her. Sam deserved to be free of her pain.

Soon the morning sun filled the room. I got Kate ready and sent her off to school. When I knew the vet’s office would be open I called and said, "I think it's time." They agreed and told me to bring her in that afternoon.

How was I going to tell Kate? Should I pick her up from school and bring her home to say goodbye to Sam? I contemplated giving Kate that opportunity, but after praying and reflecting, it seemed getting Sam to the vet’s office—alone—was the best choice. I didn’t want to have to confront the issue of a one last goodbye and the firm but painful decision to put Sam down. These were complicated explanations for such a young child to understand, and gut wrenching emotions to go through. I also knew the aftermath conversation was going to be tricky enough.

I called a friend of mine who knew about Sam's situation, and she volunteered to go to the vet's office with me. I called another friend who agreed to take Kate home with her daughter after school. I'd retrieve her when the agonizing ordeal was over.

Saying goodbye to Sam and staying with her to the end was awful. I've described her as Kate's buddy, but she was my buddy, too. Holding her as her spirit slowly left this world broke my heart. I stayed with her for a bit, taking some time to experience my own grief and sense of loss. After I said goodbye, my eyes still red from crying and with a deep ache in my heart, I began to rehearse the script I would soon deliver to Kate. If you've ever had to do this, you know how horrible I felt.

Knowing it was impossible to avoid, I not only anticipated Kate's pain, but yearned to absorb it for her. On the other hand, the old standard adages popped into my head. We've all heard about how losing pets are a part of life, kids are resilient, and we'll get through this…blah, blah, blah. Right now, none of that mattered, and did nothing to ease my grief or the pain of what I knew was coming for Kate. Taking a moment to pray and ask for guidance I knew my purpose was to be emotionally and physically present for my daughter. I was learning what servant motherhood was all about. My role was not simply to remove or avoid obstacles. I was there to here to support and help my child navigate her way through tough times.

When I arrived to pick up Kate it was all I could do to stop the tears that had already been flowing for hours. There she was sitting on the floor, busy playing and happy as a lark. With a thank you and goodbye to our friends, Kate and I headed out the door. The captivating night sky, with its glittering stars and majestic moon seemed to embrace my heavy heart, helping me to engage with the vastness of the universe and our part in God's plan.

Walking toward the car, I swallowed past the lump in my throat and slowed down. "Kate, I need to tell you about Sam." I knelt to her eye level and said, "She went to heaven today." My sweet little girl just looked at me, fell into my arms and sobbed.

After a moment she backed away from me, tilted her head towards heaven and took a deep breath. Looking up into the night sky and with no hesitation or care, she yelled, "God, I want my dog back!" Kate then fixed her gaze on me. "Where is she, Mom? Where did she go?"

I explained in simple terms that the cancer had caused Sam pain and suffering. Kate fell back into my arms. Holding each other tight we both wept. We stayed in that front yard embracing one another in the darkness until it felt right to leave.

IT CAN BE TOUGH TO FIND THE WORDS

Even for adults speaking with each other, finding the right words for sad events, heartbreaking moments, serious setbacks, and losses can be difficult. Even before being a mom, I learned to bring hardships and heartaches to prayer, asking for wisdom and for Spirit to lead me to share the right words at the right time. There is power in silence, too, so I ask for wisdom to know when sharing silence is best.

During the most difficult periods of my life, I'm so grateful that I don't have to rely only on my own wisdom to parent. Exaggerated self-reliance is one of my character flaws, so many times I've had to pray to let go and ask for grace to deal with situations. Relying only on my own resources rather than accepting help from God or others crossing my path is a recipe for disappointment and disaster. That's why I pray for humility every day. As a single mom I ran to God in my silence and in my prayers, asking for direction, comfort, and grace to let go and give it to God. I know He'll watch over me with tender love and care—just as a mother watches over her child.

NO SUCH THING AS ONE-SIZE-FITS-ALL

Helping children who are deeply hurt by disappointments or losses over which they have no control can sometimes feel overwhelming because a "one-size-fits-all" formula doesn't exist. Parents are human too, and the right words escape us at times. Sometimes silence is healing, but at other times it can feel like pretending the "bad thing" never happened. Or, on the other side, we can say too much, as if we can solve the problem or make a loss go away if we can talk until the pain miraculously vanishes.

The answer lies in being authentic and honest about our own feelings of sadness or loss. Kate was aware that she was not alone in her grief over losing Sam. It was our shared grief. The loss of a pet or a beloved grandparent, to give two examples, are childhood experiences for many people, but so far, no one has written the perfect script that makes everything okay. These situations are not okay, and as parents we know this. So do our kids. Maybe embracing our inadequacies and showing up in the moment just as we are is the best thing we can do for our kids, often with no words—no advice. We sit as companions in the silence. (This isn't so different from what we often need to do when our kids have disappointments and troubles at school or with friends and they must work through the hurt.)

At times, the loss of a loved one or a pet seems to escape our best attempt to express understanding and empathy. The child's feelings seem impenetrable. However, be honest anyway, stay open, and allow the feelings to flow. Sometimes, parents can unwittingly leave the impression that the feelings they wish their children didn't have are somehow the "wrong feelings," or even "bad" feelings. It can be a tricky concept, this notion that there is no such thing as right or wrong feelings. But our children connect with us when we allow them to feel what they feel, without judgment. This is what your child will remember in the long run. One of my favorite quotes, used earlier in the book, comes from author and poet, Maya Angelou: *People will forget what you said, people will forget what you did, but people will never forget how you made them feel.*

When it comes to parenting, we can take that quote to the bank!

Staying connected is the reason it's so important to share—embrace—your children's grief. All the emotions welling up inside are okay. Let them know what you're experiencing, too. No need to hide your emotions. Your grief and vulnerability mean your child is seeing you cope with your emotions over the same loss. Look at it this way, when children lose a grandparent, that usually means one of their parents has lost a parent or a step-parent and also is grieving. As adults we may feel the loss somewhat differently, but children can handle the idea that their parents are sad, too. When you embrace the situation, you're creating a foundation of trust and vulnerability, a platform for your children to honestly, openly share their feelings.

Brené Brown is one of my favorite inspirational women of this era. Participating in one of her courses, "Brave Leaders," opened my eyes to the value of embracing the depth of vulnerability and resiliency. This was powerful work for a servant mother. Brown reminds us that we are emotional beings, with emotions preceding thoughts. Early in my life, a forward-thinking counselor opened my understanding of my emotions. This helped me confront what I feel. Like many people, I avoided feelings, tucking them away and getting on with things. However, emotions are right on point. They are inherent internal messengers that deliver important information to our conscious rational self about what's really going on.

Once I experienced this reality for myself, I could stay in the muck of emotions with Kate and be in the feelings right along with her. We often need to practice noting and differentiating our emotions, one from the other. Anger isn't the same as fear; irritation isn't the same as rage. Being curious about feelings rather than burying them or negating them is a sign of vulnerability and maturity. Children who don't fear their feelings are free to ask questions about emotions and where their feelings come from. That can be a tough question, but it helps build connection and empathy when children realize that others have a range of emotions just like they do.

You can see this for yourself if you share your feelings with your children about a disappointment or loss that may not directly affect them. Of course, make sure it is something within the realm of their understanding. You might be surprised how well your children understand what's affecting you, perhaps even piping up with ideas of their own that help you cope with your situation.

If you're dealing with a problem that has a solution, as opposed to a loss that can't be reversed, you can ask your children for ideas about how they would handle the problem. If you have supported them when they were especially vulnerable and feeling all they feel, it's possible intuitive feelings and useful ideas will come up. Just wait and see.

Disappointments, hardships, and losses are a part of our children's reality. It's up to parents to help children adjust to this realistic impression of the world. Providing stability in our child's world is necessary and can help them develop the tools to make it through hard times, one day at a time.

THE HABIT OF PRAYER

Parents might want to shield children from losses and their struggles with difficult emotions. It is easier to do this when they're young and don't need to hear explanations they can't understand. As kids mature, we find ourselves trying to achieve a necessary, but delicate balance of appropriate protection, as we also avoid falling into overprotection. As much as we want to, we can't always soften life's blows. Teach your children to bring difficult things into their prayer lives. Start by praying with them regularly, but especially during painful times. An already written prayer or a routine prayer works but using your own words can be a wonderful prayer as you show up in the moment and speak from the heart.

Remind your children that God listens to their prayers. By the example of your habit of prayer, children learn that they are not in alone in facing their life challenges. They also will learn not to respond to questions about their well-being, or their feelings, by saying, "I got this," or "I'm fine." These are declarations that reflect an inflated attitude of self-reliance. What a blessing when our children know that God is available and listening, and they aren't expected to face everything on their own, alone. This always present God didn't create us to be alone.

MOM MEMO
In Search of the Right Thing—Saying Goodbye

- When faced with an impending or immediate loss, think carefully about how you explain the situation to your children. Taking into account their age and level of understanding, be as honest as you can.
- Recognize the value of silence, knowing we can't wipe away pain and grief simply because we want to. Being

present with your child during these hard times is sometimes the best choice.

- Learn all you can about your emotions and feel what your child feels over losses. Your children will remember that you took the time and made the effort to understand their feelings during the hardest times of their lives.
- Be kind to yourself if you struggle to find the right words during tough times. Every parent goes through this—there is no magic formula and each situation demands its own response.
- Share your struggles with your children at levels appropriate for their ages understanding, knowing that being open to talking about feelings is one of the ways children develop empathy.
- Pray for help in dealing with your children's feelings over inevitable losses in life, and help them understand they also can rely on Spirit to help them. Both through you and through prayer, your children will learn they are not alone and dependent only on themselves to cope with loss.

Blessed are they that mourn: for they shall be comforted.
—Matthew 5:4

THIRTEEN

Dress for Success

Dress how you want to be addressed...

—Bianca Fraser-Johnson, Leadership Expert

As a teen, I longed for mother-daughter shopping days. In my way of thinking, it would start with getting up early and leaving after breakfast. We'd shop until lunch and then bargain hunt some more. We'd call it a successful day if we ended the day exhausted yet satisfied with both the company and the clothes. Unfortunately, my fantasy shopping day never happened. Still, during my teenage years, summer jobs earnings would burn a hole in my pocket, and I wanted to spend a few days clothes shopping before school started. When I no longer needed school uniforms, I even looked forward to choosing new outfits. My parents didn't buy many of our clothes, so if I wanted new school outfits, I scrambled to work and save the money for them myself.

When I became a mom to a daughter, I hoped she'd love to shop, so the two of us could enjoy joint shopping expeditions.

And so she did. I especially enjoyed shopping with Kate right before school started, knowing that a few new outfits contributed to a fresh start each school year. So, after setting my budget and slotting a day on the calendar, Kate and I laid out a master shopping plan. Up early, and off we went.

Shopping with my daughter at any age was memorable, maybe because I made an effort to set a pleasant shopping tone in her early years. As the years passed, we didn't have battles or power struggles over "appropriate" clothes. For the most part, well before our shopping trips, we communicated at home about acceptable school attire. Being aware of one of the fads of a particular era, I had one simple request: No baggy sweats or pj looking bottoms. I'd likely have added other preferences if necessary. However, since the school had dress code guidelines of its own, I was covered, and Kate didn't argue about them. Fortunately, Kate had good taste, so I wasn't forced to declare other items off-limits. Overall, my message to Kate was, as the saying goes: Dress for success.

One morning Kate put on oversized sweatpants and a sweat-shirt. "Can I just wear this today?" she asked. Needless to say the conversation headed in the direction of a simple response: No. This outfit denoted tired or overly relaxed. I also wasn't buying into "the whole school is wearing them" response. Sure, I could have made an exception, but from day one of her teenage years, we had an agreement based on principle, namely the guidelines the school and what the two of us established. I listened to her rationale about why the sweats were okay, after which I explained my reasons for saying no. "Your closet is filled with plenty of nice clothes you picked out when we shopped at the beginning of the school year, and I liked your choices." Then I added, "Dress for success. You're setting a tone for yourself and the day ahead based on what you wear."

Kate, always a conscientious student, produced good academic results. She'd formed a strong habit and showing up every day—mentally, physically and spiritually. I still have no doubt that her school-appropriate clothing helped. Although I believe in reward and acknowledgment of a job well done, I continued to nix the sweatpants and sweatshirt.

"But why?" Kate pleaded before she proceeded to list the reasons she should be allowed to wear the old baggy sweats.

I avoided saying, "Because I said so." I'd made a commitment to myself never to utter that phrase, and I'm happy to say I never have. After hearing it way too much as a child, I loathed those words. Delving into my past, conversations and possible compromises didn't exist in our household, so "because I said so" signaled the end of a conversation. Not feeling heard—acknowledged—triggered frustration and resentment. Even looking back, I believe I had pretty valid reasons behind why I should be able to do something, but there was no time to listen.

At a parenting presentation some years ago, I heard the following: *Parenthood shouldn't be a power play between you and your child. Take time to listen to your child during times of negotiation, even if you believe you have already made up your mind about a pending decision.* That message stuck. Critical to my servant motherhood role, I committed myself to listen, engage in a dialogue, and be open to compromise. In the case of Kate's baggy clothes, I heard her reasons for being allowed to dress down, but in the end, I felt strongly about adhering to the dress code we'd already discussed. Still, I listened without interrupting and remained open-minded. After a brief exchange, Kate and I compromised. Kate owned what we might call a fashionable sweat suit, the typical jacket and matching pants, but nicer than oversize and shapeless. She switched her outfit for the day, and we were on our way to another dress-for-success day.

. . .

WHY IS THIS IMPORTANT?

Now, I'm no fashionista, but I like clothes and I take pride in what I wear. I have childhood memories involving clothes, some pleasant, some I'd rather forget. One fond memory involves my dad and his weekly shoe-polishing frenzy. I attended Catholic elementary middle school and wore a uniform, so my only clothing choice was picking out a new pair of shoes at the start of each school year. My brothers and sister and I went together to our local shoe store where my mom patiently waited for four kids to get sized and then pick out a pair of leather shoes. It was our responsibility to keep them clean and intact, for they were intended to last the entire school year. That meant shoe maintenance was a ritual at our house.

Every Sunday night, my dad sat in his living chair and we'd place our shoes at his feet. Then he'd clean and polish five pairs of shoes, his and ours. This Sunday night ritual lasted through middle school. When we were old enough to do this job on our own, my dad looked down at our shoes and gave us a hard time if they weren't polished to his standards. This was a simple self-care ritual for our expensive shoes, the only school fashion investment we had. That was the extent of my wardrobe selection for some time, but it was a valuable exercise in routine self-care.

As a servant mom, I believed that when Kate headed off to school, it was important that she feel confident and, borrowing the phrase linked to business, dressed for success. I saw self-esteem as including an element wrapped up in a package of how one dresses. What we wear both asks and answers the question: Do I care enough about myself to dress appropriately? This isn't about money, because our clothing doesn't need to be either expensive or ostentatious. Dressing for success really means showing confidence, an "I care" attitude that communicates self-worth through how we treat our personal "outside package." It sends the first impression, that almost instantaneous reaction from others, and telegraphs clues about what we think of ourselves.

Viewed in context, the idea of dressing for success isn't the least bit trivial. Job interviews, social occasions, and other events require appropriate clothing choices. In my management and executive positions, it was my job to interview young adult candidates for potential job openings. Countless times I was surprised, even shocked by the way an interviewee was dressed; those reactions formed my first impression. Jeans, T-shirts, and leggings often set the tone for the first meeting with a person in a position to move them through the employment process or set aside their application. Did these thoughtlessly dressed young men and women take themselves or the potential job seriously? How could I take them seriously?

Obviously, all kinds of reasons come to mind that explain why some young, and not so young, people are not just poorly dressed, but seem unaware of what's appropriate attire. That's why I'd give them the benefit of the doubt, and often hire those who were otherwise a good fit for the position. Maybe they'd never heard the dress for success message. I was careful not to pass judgement on a young candidate, not knowing what may or may not be in their closet. As a mom, a former teacher, and a youth advocate, I'd hope that someone, somewhere along the journey would share particulars about the interviewing process, including dress.

Whether it's a first job interview or an interview for an upper level position, appropriate dress is important. This is why men and women of all ages might joke with each other about their "interview suit." When they buy a new suit, it usually replaces the old interview suit. I'd often use interview situations as a teaching moment, an opportunity to tell the candidates the importance of dress in leaving a first impression. At the very least, I provided a tool for the new hire to use in the future.

I believe that many of us have noticed that in the recent years, perhaps related to changes occurring during the COVID-19 pandemic, the regular dress codes for small, local restaurants are nonexistent. Unless there's a uniform, like fast food restaurants require, many employers are pleased to have enough staff and don't push other agendas, like dress codes or uniforms. I wouldn't define leggings as work pants in most situations, or baggy jeans, for that matter, but for whatever reason, they seem to be okay work attire right now and a T-shirt often finishes out the outfit. If I were talking to young person applying for a restaurant job, I would still advise wearing better clothing. If that means they stand out to customers, so much the better.

SHOPPING ISN'T WHAT IT USED TO BE

It's possible shopping malls will soon be relics of the past, and online clothes shopping will become the new norm. But even if we rarely step foot in brick and mortar stores, we need to create a process or a ritual around shopping with our children. Parents will still need to balance needs and wants based on circumstances and what's reasonable. Regardless of shopping method, allow your children to be a part of the process. First, create a clothing budget. With older children, decide if they'll contribute money to the dollar amount available. If they're working, how much of their earnings are saved or put to other essential uses, and what dollar amount can they spend on clothes? When young people invest real money in their looks, they're more likely to respect the value of their clothes and take care of them.

Before you step foot in the mall or open the website, establish boundaries for acceptable clothing styles. This isn't about control. It's about an opportunity to address self-respect along with supporting self-expression and creativity. It begins to imprint the notion of dressing for success and communicates your awareness. Once the parameters are set, allow your child to create a look. Never mind that you wouldn't wear it. Offer support for their choices—be free with compliments about how they appear in the clothing. They care what their peers think, but they also long for approval from mom or dad.

DRESS FOR SUCCESS

Before I had Kate, I was a high school teacher and attended typical teacher training workshops. One workshop focused on the influence of teenage dress in schools, particularly clothing that potentially identified groups or possible gangs. We were taught to look for identifiers to help isolate the groups or avoid their development in the first place. I quickly learned of the signals and outward signs, such as how a particular article of clothing was worn, and what that communicated to potential members. Hats, pants, baseball caps, belts and so on, sent an identifying message to other members or potential members inside and outside of school. Baseball caps could be tipped to the right or to the left, or worn backwards, all of which differentiated various groups/gangs from each other. How one's pants were "hung" on their waist, low, uneven, or beltless provided another insider message. Even knowing Kate wasn't dressing to send messages to a specific group, it became even clearer that clothing fads and styles create a culture. More than any other group, teenagers want to fit in and tend to dress like others in their "pack." Mirroring, as it's called, offers a sense of security, and if we look at a teenager's crowd, we see patterns in their fashion.

Psychologists also tell us we tend to dress in tune with how we feel. I believe this, because I've experienced it. I might go to the closet and pull out a particular outfit, but then decide it doesn't match what I am feeling that day. I head back into the closet and make another choice or change what I'm already wearing. Maybe something colorful will lift a low mood or a favorite jacket will make me feel professional and in charge. In the 1980s, the term "power suit" came into use, especially among women. The concept is rooted in women's struggle to be taken seriously in what at the time were male dominated fields.

Regardless of its origins, the idea of clothing having power and influence has had staying power and has evolved over time. It's based on the idea that we choose what we wear for subtle, often unconscious reasons. The looser items we choose might follow a holiday binge or recent celebration with lots of food. We moms are masters of a fashion consciousness that fits our life and energy, while also reinforcing our positive intentions. What servant mom wouldn't want this for her child?

WHAT WE WEAR, WHAT WE DO

Clothes not only project an outward message, but they also affect the way we perform. I was intrigued to learn about the concept of "enclosed cognition." Researchers at Northwestern University discovered that the clothing we wear affects not only our psychological states, but our performance levels. I didn't have this resource in my pocket when I told Kate, "How you dress is how you'll perform," but it makes sense. I could relate to this concept myself. I could identify times that my performance was subpar, because I'd dressed down, relaxed my usual standard. I learned quickly that I was more productive and focused if I dressed like I meant business.

During the COVID-19 pandemic, other mothers told me about the challenge of being ready for the homeschooling routine, which meant getting out of pajamas and into school appropriate clothes. Smart move. It was a trying and unprecedented time across the country, so consistency and as much normalcy in routines as possible was important. When getting dressed remained part of the routine, then it likely seemed at least somewhat "normal" to show up at the computer at the appointed time.

WHO AM I?

As a servant mom, it was important to encourage Kate to be her own person and to express herself, and clothing choice allows for individuality, just as choosing activities and friends are self-expression and needed to come from her. Parameters—boundaries—gave her a framework of accountability for her actions and decisions. The truth is we all function better with parameters and boundaries, along with accountability. As a parent it's important to remain the parent and set realistic expectations for your children, while recognizing the internal struggle to find their places in this world.

Watching Kate mature and move into her own space, I also recognized that she embraced her sensuality, her womanhood, rather than avoiding it or running away from it. Shopping for a special occasion like prom or a wedding reception, she was comfortable with her body. When I say this, I mean embracing her femininity and tastefully choosing a dress or shirt that accentuated her beauty, rather than shielding it or covering it up. Her choices were tasteful, beautiful, and age appropriate. I noticed this because I didn't have that level of confidence at age eighteen.

My mom wasn't with me when I shopped for a prom dress, homecoming pageant gown, or wedding dress. But it went deeper than that. I didn't discuss growing girlhood pains with my mom, which resulted in insecurity about my body and being. I also addressed that issue in counseling and learned to love and embrace the woman I was and who I would become.

Preparing children to launch into the world is our job, which is why I advise you to set boundaries, stay strong in your convictions, and be their parent, not their friend. If you listen to their attempts to compromise or share the reasoning behind their ideas, you'll avoid a power trip and the need to be right. Much of the time, discussion and compromise lead you toward a win-win outcome. When especially difficult decisions come up, make them as the parent in charge, demonstrating conviction and a commitment to being as fair as possible.

WHAT IS YOUR INTENTION?

I intended to raise Kate to understand and embrace the concept of gratitude. As part of that, she learned the value of money and setting goals to earn money, work hard, and then enjoy the fruits of her labor. As a component of gratitude, paying herself first by saving, but also tithing, kept her aware of those less fortunate. We also didn't focus on material things, monetary rewards, or what we lacked, but were grateful for what we had. Clothing choice was just an example of a blessing we had, plus the option to change clothes each day.

I taught Kate to respect the value of money by understanding price points, making a dollar stretch, looking for bargains, and understanding quality over quantity. Kate and I talked about what portion of her money she would spend on clothes. Finance was not one of my strongest skills, but as a single mom I quickly learned to make it a priority. Kate learned what it was to establish a budget, contribute to investment accounts, and avoid a paycheck-to-paycheck mindset or lifestyle. I wanted money talk to have a positive tone in our home.

Money and finances can be a painful topic for single moms when money is always tight and a never-ending source of concern. I was committed to keeping grown up conversations about money out of Kate's earshot. Even one- or two-parent families who aren't skirting poverty can feel tensions around money. That was true for me, and it's why I took such a different path with Kate. As a kid, I experienced the tension, but I never had facts that filled in the picture. It always seemed we struggled as a family of six. I formed that opinion mostly from absorbing the arguments between my parents, which often were around money. This taught me not to ask for anything unless it was a necessity or beyond my meager financial means. This meant creatively looking for ways to earn the money in order to take advantage of an opportunity to go to a movie or out to eat with friends.

Counseling helped me discover that I'd developed financial responsibility at a very young age, primarily because I was afraid to ask my mom and dad for anything. This came from sensing the tension around money, making it a topic I didn't want to approach with my parents. I remember heading out to dinner as a family and ordering the cheapest thing on a menu whether I liked it or not. As a kid, I thought that might help the piggy bank. As time marched on I embraced the concept of financial responsibility and paid for many things, including college tuition and my wedding.

My parents paid for certain necessities, but I developed the mindset not to ask for anything above and beyond what I thought was essential. It brought on angst and internal agitation that was difficult to grasp at a young age. Over the long haul, I dreaded spending money out of fear the reservoir would run dry. Fortunately, I sought help. I'm the mom and woman I am today because of my journey and commitment to finding a way to resolve issues and to work to make things happen, from career moves to effectively managing money. I am grateful for that and the tenacity this life experience taught me. If I wanted something, I worked for it. With determination, a bit of blood, sweat, and tears and lots of prayers, I found a way to make things happen.

A healthy relationship with money helped me as a servant mom and it has contributed to the resilient, survivor, entrepreneurial mom I became. Part of my life lesson was learning how to balance saving for the future, and while staying within my means, to enjoy all that life has to offer. All work and no play don't make for a happy mom.

SPEAKING OF SHOPPING...

Shopping isn't always about clothes, and I recall a shopping trip that almost never happened, mainly because Kate decided to try out a little "attitude" on me. She was in second grade and had been invited to her best friend's birthday party. She was excited about the upcoming festivities with Laura and other friends and asked me about getting a birthday present for Laura.

One evening after work, I asked Kate about going to the mall after dinner to find Laura a gift. She was eager to go, so I prepared dinner and told Kate we'd head to the mall when we finished dinner. Kate ate most of her dinner but wanted something other than the salad.

"When you finish your salad, we will head to the mall," I said. I moved a few steps away to the kitchen to clean up the dishes, and it was then that some whining began with, "I don't want my salad."

"That's the last of dinner, so finish up, and we'll get out of here."

Kate left her chair holding her salad bowl and approached me. Showing a sassy attitude she said, "Well, why don't you just eat my salad?"

Her little attitude surprised me, and I had to hold back a smile as I realized she was testing the waters of respect. I reached for her hand, the one holding the bowl. "Do not speak to me that way." Salad flew up in the air and rained down onto the kitchen floor.

Kate quickly dropped the bowl on the kitchen counter and said, "Oh my gosh, what am I doing? Oh, why did I say that?" She ran down the hall to her bedroom and slammed the door.

I was in the kitchen cleaning up the salad from the floor and smiling inside about her attempt to push boundaries with me. I was pretty sure she was testing out some of the attitudes she'd seen in some of her classmates and thought she would try it out on her mom. But I had zero tolerance for backtalk and a bad attitude.

After a few minutes, I approached her room and opened the door. Kate hopped off her bed and said, "I'm so sorry, I'm so sorry. I don't know why I said that."

We hugged, and I told her I didn't appreciate the attitude and sassy response. "Maybe you can speak to your friends that way but don't you ever speak to me or any adult that way."

We cleaned up and went shopping.

I could go on and on about this, but the bottom line is that she knew about being respectful and that bad attitudes didn't carry any weight in our home. I never had an issue with Kate and her attitude from when she was in second grade until she left for college. Sure, we had our back and forth conversations, and we didn't agree on everything, but if you want to earn respect, you must give it.

Kate understood reciprocity, giving and receiving respect. Regardless of her age, I showed her respect by taking time to listen, be attentive, and create a safe space to share her feelings when she needed and wanted to. We shared mutual respect.

WHAT CLOTHES SHOPPING CAN LEAD TO

This entire discussion started with clothes shopping and the way it became such a thing for Kate and me. More than simply looking for an outfit for Kate, shopping became about gratitude for having the means to do it. I expressed humility in having the ability to buy clothes for a new school year, a meaningful act many of us associate with new beginnings. We consciously spoke about her need for clothes and the guidelines I put forward, and then we fully enjoyed our time together. Some of these trips led to stories and occasions to recall other shopping adventures with Kate, from looking for a prom dress to shopping for her wedding gown.

My rule as servant mother continually taps into gratitude and humility. I was always grateful to God for good health and the means to support my child. Every day we are reminded of others who are struggling. As a woman of faith I believe in tithing, and acts of kindness are important life lessons I shared with Kate.

When I was in middle school, my friend Wendy and I were in choir together. While preparing for our spring concert one year, the director asked if we could all wear spring clothes in light colors for our concert. We were excited with ideas and the opportunity to shop for a new shirt or skirt. My attention, along with a few other students, was directed toward Wendy. She came from a strict religious household that didn't celebrate holidays or birthdays, which limited opportunities for new clothes or gift exchanges. Well aware of Wendy's situation, the director proposed that we chip in and buy Wendy an outfit for the concert. Being respectful of her family's traditions, we were able to present this to her as a "just because" gesture. It was unanimous and we collected small donations from each student in our class and bought a simple, spring outfit for Wendy.

I'll always remember the day we presented the outfit to Wendy. With tears in her eyes and a big grin she humbly said thank you. She headed to the locker room to try it on quickly, returning to rousing applause. It was easy to appreciate how good she felt in her new clothes, because she beamed from the inside out. No doubt this incident had a profound impact on her self-esteem and overall demeanor. I once shared this story with Kate, emphasizing the happiness and simplicity in this small gesture of kindness that had such a huge impact, not only on Wendy but on the class as a whole. I also never forgot the kindness and attentiveness our teacher showed.

NO LACK OF OPPORTUNITIES

When Kate was eight-months-old, she journeyed with me to Ashland, Kentucky, alongside thirty Church youth group members. We were headed to Ashland to build houses with Habitat for Humanity. On the first day of a seven-day work project, we met Michael, one of ten kids, living outside the city limits of Ashland in a shanty with his family. Michael rode his bike barefoot to the worksite every day dressed in dirty shorts and a torn T-shirt. He was what the high school boys called an irritant at times, giving them advice and commenting on the work pace. However, Michael's behavior sent an important message of wanting to be involved—and included.

In no time, Michael moved himself quickly into the hearts of the youth and became a part of the team. As the week ended, one of the youth group members posed the question, "How about if we buy Michael a pair of shoes and maybe some shorts and a T shirt?" We had some money made from previous fund-raising events that we were going to donate to Habitat and to the local church that housed us for the week. The teens suggested we use some of these funds to outfit Michael. What a great idea. We asked if it was possible to extend this gesture to Michael and were given the go ahead. Our teenagers shopped and bought Michael a pair of shorts, a T-shirt, and a pair of sneakers. When we presented these gifts to him, he was speechless, awkwardly slumping into the arms of one of the burly male teens for a hug. Emotions were raw for all as Michael revealed his tender heart and quiet gratitude.

A simple pair of shoes and new clothes changed him, but also touched the lives of the teens on our team as well. The next day we packed up the vans to head home, and Michael came to the worksite to say goodbye dressed in his new outfit and shoes. His smiling face radiated with pride and gratitude. The teenagers did as well. As our two vans drove away from the worksite, Michael waved goodbye to our two vans full of teary high school students. Michael stood below the twelve-foot Habitat sign that read, "God's people helping God's people." Michael had a lifelong memory, and so did the teenagers. All involved carried away a reminder of the importance of service and generosity.

A servant mom wants to provide the best for her children of course. In doing the best we can, we also want to send the message about helping others, sharing the concept of gratitude and paying it forward. It creates a new pathway towards making a difference. Clothes can do that! It's an outward sign that tells us about others and ourselves. Like the Good Samaritan, feeding and clothing those less fortunate is our call as Christians. Sharing was a ritual in our house. In a spirit of love and compassion, we donated clothes that no longer fit or we didn't wear anymore. I recall folding some freshly laundered shirts with Kate at my side and carefully packing them in a bag or box with the heartfelt intention that someone would benefit from this slightly used gift.

BEYOND DRESSING FOR SUCCESS

Obviously, it takes more than clothes to be successful. But how we dress is often an outward sign of what's going inside. In our culture, clothes are powerful. They say a lot about who are kids are. Think of the theater and think of how costumes both help create and complete a character. This is true for your children. Have a say in at least steering them in the right direction when they're developing a personal style, while also help them avoid what could be so-called fashion statements they may soon regret.

MOM MEMO
Dress for Success

- Care what your teens wear. Show interest and pay attention to how they're expressing themselves.
- Set parameters around a dress code for your youngsters, and do it sooner rather than later—you're a parent, not a friend.
- Support your children's desire to create their own fashion sense. It may not resemble yours, but their styles are an extension of who they are.
- Compliment their choices: the color, the design, the beauty in the look they create. At any age, they need to hear these things from you.

- Be honest if you don't like the look. If they're insistent on a specific type of clothing, discuss their reasons and perhaps find a compromise.
- Have fun with shopping. Take a day and shop with the idea that you'll try on anything, especially items you think you'll never wear. Do it together. Laugh and enjoy the craziness. You may end up finding you like something you never imagined wearing.
- Talk about clothing as it relates to their next chapter in life, perhaps an interview for a job or an internship or scholarship. Don't assume they're getting that information from their schools. You are also an important resource.

To me clothing is a form of self-expression. There are hints about who you are in what you wear.

—Marc Jacobs, Fashion Designer

FOURTEEN

The Art of the Thank You Note

Appreciation can make a day, even change a Life. Your willingness to put it into words is all that is necessary.

—Margaret Cousins, Author, Editor

Growing up, "please" and "thank you" were a part of everyday life. Mom and Dad were sticklers about respect, which included etiquette and manners. Their introduction to proper behavior created a foundation for what would later morph into an attitude of gratitude and appreciation.

Please and thank you came with every request, especially every acceptance of a display of generosity, from compliments and gifts to fulfilled requests. It's just how it was. I'm grateful for that lesson, which made me a manner-minded person and mom myself. From the beginning, teaching Kate to add thank you and please to her vocabulary and use them when fitting became a mantra, and I reciprocated when speaking to her, demonstrating that respect and gratitude work both ways. My message to my daughter was that she would never be too old or too proud to use those simple but powerful words.

Enter the art of the thank you note, which sadly could be fading into oblivion unless we revive it. Elsewhere, I've discussed the value of a handwritten note, but the written thank you note deserves its own mention. As a child, these notes took on a life of their own during the holidays and on our birthdays. Christmas vacation signaled it was time to create our list of people and write thank you notes to everyone who remembered us at Christmas. My brothers, sister, and I would gather at the dining room table with notepaper and pencil or pen in hand and begin working down our lists. With our large Irish/Italian Catholic extended family, the lists were long, especially because they also included family friends. If they remembered us in the smallest way, their name was added to the thank you note list.

As I recall, the notes were quite structured, and I also remember taking extreme care with those sent to my one Nana, a retired schoolteacher. She expected that notes to her would be written in cursive. Then, after expressing her appreciation for the thank you note, she gently shared commentary on our penmanship in the form of "well done" or "needs improvement." Either way, I didn't mind, because our conversations with her always included valuable lessons.

From those early days until now, every chapter of my life has been punctuated by the please and thank you mindset. I still acknowledge generous and thoughtful acts, from meal invitations to a birthday card. Especially nowadays, who doesn't enjoy getting something other than advertising or bills? It's fun to open a card that arrives via snail mail.

In general, letter writing is somewhat of a lost art. It's no longer an ordinary skill learned in childhood. However, we can make a different choice. Why not intentionally make a thank you note part of the communication and relationship building foundation we build for our children?

KEEPING IT SIMPLE

I intended to pass this gratitude mindset and habit on to my daughter for many reasons. Along with instilling positive values and displaying manners, I was confident this habit would serve her well in her personal *and* professional life. I kept the teaching end simple. A request was followed with *please,* and acceptance of any gift, complement, or gracious gesture received a *thank you,* either verbal or written.

Holiday and birthday good wishes or congratulatory gifts were followed up with Kate's thank you notes. That was how this cornerstone in Kate's life was reinforced throughout her childhood. The message to Kate was gratitude, along with my belief that we should never take anything for granted.

A thank you note is a visible way to show gratitude for all the gifts in our lives. Cultivating an attitude of gratitude helps us recognize even the small gifts or wins in life. It also presents an opportunity to look for gratitude even in the midst of difficulties. Sometimes we need to dig deep to summon a spirit of gratitude. Tough times are only temporary, and they too provide a lesson. With a God-centered approach to life, I was clear that He never promised us a life free of challenges. And this was true of parenting as well. With a God-centered approach to parenting, I learned I wasn't alone in servant motherhood, which gave me confidence and gratitude for all circumstances in my life. This was not easy at times, but I had faith in the outcome, whatever it was, and learned to be grateful even in the most challenging times as a mother.

It isn't mentioned often enough, but being thankful, even for challenges, contributes to feelings of happiness and contentment. This isn't only true for me, but is a well-accepted principle in the "art of living." For me, a state of appreciation reflects how I see the world and often changes the way I look at things. When we focus on gratitude, we're naturally less self-focused or self-centered.

As part of my role as a servant mother, I wanted—needed—to set an example for Kate in how we act during difficult times. Sure, I expressed disappointment and frustration when the bottom fell out of well-laid plans or something upset me. However, I then moved into a place where I looked for the lesson in the fallout or disappointment, which then helped me stay positive and express gratitude for the lesson and for what mattered. This was a model for Kate. No negative Nelly! Instead, I hoped to instill a richer, more profound appreciation for life and all the small things. I wanted Kate to develop the ability to express gratitude for the people, things and experiences life threw her way, no matter the outcome.

It may not seem obvious, but writing a thank you note helps kids understand *why* they are thankful. This gesture, a sign of respect and an acknowledgment, helps them move deeper into this space. Making a thank you note a part of a giving and receiving ritual is a way to model a consciousness of gratitude. As Kate matured, it was satisfying to see that she understood what gratitude meant and felt good about it. She also learned to be specific about her gratitude, rather than spout generalizations that can sound like platitudes.

THE WORDS MATTER

Like many parents do, I repeated thank you and please to my daughter at a young age in hopes they'd be words she'd learn early and say back to me. I recall the times when, as toddlers often do, she'd share a piece of her lunch with me, and I'd put my hand over my heart and express a heartfelt thank you. Since saying please and thank you were almost instinctual for me, thanks to my parents, being a role model for Kate in this expression of gratitude was natural—and necessary. It was special when I first heard Kate mimic my words and direct them to me. My heart filled with joy for this simple but priceless gift.

FROM FIRST WORDS TO FIRST NOTES

It's not a big leap to go from a toddler's cute pleases and thank-yous to written notes, a process I guided all through Kate's childhood. The importance of thank you notes was validated during my daughter's senior year of high school. Her English teacher devoted a class session or two to what he called "the lost art of the thank you note." Mr. S specifically discussed the near demise of thank you notes and he was wise enough to tell the class that these notes could be important in their careers. Sending a thank you note after an interview, an audition, or an invitation to a business function isn't some meaningless gesture, but should be well thought out and intentional. If the note expresses genuine sincerity, it's possible it could influence a potential business decision—really. It always leaves an impression and in some cases, the note-sender stands out when other opportunities come along.

Mr. S's assignment was to write thank you notes to various individuals. Kate got kind of a kick out of this assignment because it was old hand for her. The teacher stressed that it was up to them to keep this nearly lost art alive, while also remembering the importance of sharing and expressing gratitude.

When Kate was in college, she sent a thank you note to Mr. S., who in turn sent her a note to thank her for acknowledging what he'd taught. It must have been gratifying for him to know that his ideas stuck.

TODAY'S CHALLENGES

The power of gratitude and thankful hearts can never be underestimated. So, servant mom, how are the thank yous and pleases in your life? Without a doubt, we're immersed in world that is me-centered, and our kids and teens live in this atmosphere whether they created it or not. For this reason, try to be a solid role model for building a grateful heart and a living space where thankfulness dwells. Teach your kids respect and honor others by saying please and thank you to them. Be a role model letting them see you behave that way in your work-life, with friends, and family. As a volleyball coach and a teacher, I used please and thank you with my players and students.

By the way, when you show children respect, you aren't compromising your authority—and the same is true in your workplace. Unfortunately, some people believe that much like offering apologies, using please and thank you shows weakness. This simply isn't true, and it's a nearly-dead idea from the past anyway. In my experience, respect and appreciation bring better results than a barking authoritative directive. The statistics bear this out. If you're in a managerial or supervisory role, you're aware that retaining employees is better than losing them, and retention is influenced by how appreciated someone feels. Respect begets respect in virtually every human interaction.

Your children will be employees someday and will likely find themselves in a leadership role, big or small, in whatever field they choose. All the more reason to teach them the please and thank you attitude now. Most parents start developing this respectful attitude when they ask a young child to *please take out the trash* or *please clear the table,* then say a sincere *thank you* when the task is done. These everyday requests build a habit over time.

IT DOESN'T HAVE TO BE A CHORE

For a young child, writing thank you notes can be an exercise in self-expression. You can supply special paper, perhaps brightly colored and later, even monogrammed, or you can help them create a special decorated message with stickers or stamps. Provide colored pens or pencils or markers. Let them know early on that saying thank you isn't a dry, dull, "have to" chore but a chance to have a little fun too. You're helping to birth a lifelong habit and a positive attitude to match.

In a few years, they'll be zipping notes off after job interviews or to thank someone for a kind act, or they'll send a note to a friend just because. Cards and personal letters tend to be saved, reread, and cherished for years to come. With any luck, someday your mailbox will have a thank you note from your child.

A NOVEL IDEA

As a confidence or self-esteem builder, try having your children write a thank you note to themselves that highlights the positive qualities they see. Make sure they understand this is a private letter—for their eyes only. If they need suggestions, talk about your gratitude for them, highlighting qualities authentically theirs—bright eyes, uplifting smile, sense of humor, or how their brain works to solve the most challenging math problems. Encourage them to think about people, places, and things that have come along and enriched their lives.

When they're done, they can seal their letters in an envelope and address it to themselves and give it to you for safekeeping. Then, as inevitably happens, they'll soon hit a rough patch that might challenge their outlook, attitude, and ultimately, their gratitude. They could have tough days at school navigating peer pressure, and growing pains might rattle their confidence for who they are.

It's possible that your children lack gratitude at the moment. Or, a trickle or a flood of cognitive thoughts loop through their mind, and they believe these negative thoughts about themselves or their world. As nurturing servant moms, we don't want our children to treat these negative thoughts as fact. That's where gratitude can come in. Gratitude changes attitudes. Some may discover this easily, but for others it will take longer to develop and will need practice and repetition.

If you see a negative mindset developing, take out the letter and mail it. In a day or two it will show up in the mailbox. Give the kids the space to open the thank you note and read it privately. They will receive a gentle reminder of their inner beauty and strengths that no one can take that away and bad days can't abolish. They will be reminded of the "thank you" qualities they possess.

THE THANKFUL STATE OF MIND

Being thankful is a state of mind, ultimately a way of life built on recognizing and giving credence to things we take for granted. When I was in grade school, my dad would wake us up to prepare for the day. Sleepy-eyed and heading to the bathroom, he would turn towards us with his shaving cream beard and sing, "How are you this morning?" In call and response fashion, we'd sing or say the line from the song, "Very well, I thank you." Then "Ding, dong, ding" would finish the nursery rhyme song. No matter what I was feeling, I answered with a positive response.

Dad had made up his own lines to the popular children's tune, "Frere Jacques," and I believed them. If we pouted or grumbled about having to get up to go to school, my dad would say, "You thank God that you can get out of bed and put both feet on the floor and have another day to play." A simple statement with a lot of punch, and I still remember it every day of my life.

From the beginning, I wanted Kate to understand the simple ways to express thanksgiving and gratitude each day. As you know, this can be an uphill battle in a society that presses upon the notion that more of something means happiness. But remaining consistent and sincere in acknowledging the simplicity of gratitude is a powerful lesson for kids. When gratitude is the operator of our lives, it's a game changer. This is true for the gifts and graces as well as for the tribulations and triumphs

Isn't it odd that a simple thank you note is one step on a path that builds heart-centered gratitude we can fall back on during difficult times? Challenges and disappointments as children provide life lessons and growth that form a baseline for how we embrace future challenges. This baseline establishes positivity and thankfulness for what we have rather than negativity over what we don't have.

From our adult perspective, we likely know firsthand that gratitude maximizes happiness. Likewise, a grateful child equals a happy child. A principle worth remembering. Faith-based gratitude provides comfort that we are not alone, and gratitude is the ability to give thanks for the things we have, the people we love and more. Gratitude is a measure of our faith, demonstrating that we are aware of the gifts God has given us, in any circumstances, which teaches our children that even in challenging times, we still look to display gratitude. They can see us embracing change and fortifying our resilience with gratitude. When we offer thanksgiving to God, we give Him enjoyment and our hearts are full when we express our thanks for all He has given us.

For some, writing thank you notes and learning basic respect and etiquette can move to another level and may result in gratitude lists and journals, which solidify in our minds the things we need to be grateful for each day.

MOM MEMO
The Art of the Thank You Note

- As conscientious moms, we can teach our kids genuine gratitude by expressing it in a variety of ways.
- Noting what you're grateful for on a daily basis can become a way of life, which is why it's a habit worth cultivating in your children.
- Writing a thank you note to another person is one valuable way to show gratitude, so start by providing the tools—paper, pens, and so on, appropriate to the age. It won't morph into a dreaded chore if it's a fun project.
- Have your kids write a private thank you note to themselves—try this strategy and see if it helps your kids move through and past tough times.
- Don't forget to tell your kids how thankful you are for them—say it often.

- Parent with the knowledge that gratitude is a game changer throughout life.

It is not joy that makes us grateful;
it is gratitude that makes us joyful.
—Brother David Steindl-Rast, a Benedictine monk

FIFTEEN

Can We Get a Puppy, Please?

Dogs are forever in the moment. They are always a tidal wave of feelings, and every feeling is some variant of love.

—Jack Canfield, Motivational Speaker

When Kate was in elementary school, we considered getting another dog. Kate was happy with our adopted kitten, Mat-the-Cat, but from time to time she'd asked for a puppy. In an earlier chapter, I talked about losing Samantha, our golden retriever, to aggressive cancer at age seven. Although some time had passed, I wasn't sure we were ready for another dog. Still, I was compelled to contact Samantha's breeder Kathy to find out if the dog's bloodline had an elevated cancer incidence. She appreciated my call, but said none of Samantha's siblings' owners had reported an occurrence of cancer. We ended the call with Kathy inviting me to contact her if we decided to get another dog. But the time wasn't right.

A few years passed, and because of work-related moves we found ourselves back in New England. The occasional mention of a dog had resurfaced as a frequent plea: "Oh please, Mom, can't we get a dog?" We now had two cats, Mat and Rocky, but they were not a dog. No one had to tell me about the added responsibility. I was acutely aware of it, but crazy endeavor or not, I, too, wanted a dog in our home.

Along with a pet comes shared responsibility. By then Kate was older, and with greater maturity, she was responsible enough to take on a puppy and contribute to its care. I also was aware of the companionship, joy, and love a dog would bring to our home. With Kate being an only child, this puppy would provide a buddy for Kate while also teaching her selflessness and unconditional love. Of course, Kate wasn't the only one that would benefit from such companionship! I was confident that Kate's commitment would go beyond lip service, even after the honeymoon phase was over. Nonetheless, I could come up with plenty of reasons why I should talk myself out of this puppy idea.

TAKING FIRST STEPS

With puppy possibilities churning in my head, I contacted Kathy, the breeder in nearby Massachusetts and told her we were considering another dog. She mentioned a new litter would arrive in six weeks, which was bait enough to seriously consider another golden retriever. Kate was ecstatic when I shared the news. My mom instincts immediately had me pivot to the old script: "Remember, having a pet is a big responsibility." Naturally, Kate had all the right answers about helping to take care of our puppy, but honestly, what child doesn't when a yes or no answer is on the line? She wanted a dog.

Weeks later, the breeder called to tell us the golden retriever puppies had arrived and would be ready to take home in eight weeks. Meanwhile, we could come to look at the new furballs if we'd like. *If?* A few weeks later we headed north, off on what I understood to be a "dangerous" adventure. Excitement and joy oozed from every fiber of Kate's being, but without hesitation, I described this trip as a fact-finding mission, an opportunity to learn about the adventures and responsibilities of taking care of a new puppy. "I'll need your help if this is going to work. We have to do this together, Kate." (I'm pretty sure I was saying all this to myself in a futile effort to talk myself out of getting a dog.)

Before we left the house, I handed Kate a pad and pen and encouraged her to write down questions for the breeder. "Pretend you're a newspaper reporter. Ask Kathy lots of questions about taking care of a new dog." Kate eagerly agreed. Of course, she did. At this point, I wasn't admitting to the possibility that we'd own a puppy, but I was ready enough to embrace the first step and begin the process of window shopping for one. Anyone who has ever decided to just "look" at puppies knows it's a dangerous proposition.

The puppies were a few weeks old when we embarked on our journey to Agawam, Massachusetts, to pay them a visit. We drove up the driveway to the kennel built on a hill as part of a well-groomed farm and long-time family dog breeding business. Renovated barns with expansive, tailored kennels housed several litters of puppies and their moms. Kathy met us and motioned for us to follow her to the barn. Within minutes Kate and I met the puppies. Full of life, the puppies gave us so much attention. We were wallowing in it. What beauties!

When we finished puppy playtime, Kathy invited us back to the house, where we sat in the family room sipping lemonade. Kate proceeded with her list of questions, showing a genuine desire to secure a puppy of her own. I sat across from her, not saying a word while the breeder answered all our questions in a straightforward and honest manner. She also reciprocated and asked

Kate about her activities, work schedule, time away from the house, and so on. It was clear she was committed to finding good homes for these puppies and had made that her business for years. She left no doubt that Kate's commitment to care for the puppy was a factor in her decision. Most importantly, Kathy was opening Kate's eyes to other commitments. She emphasized that puppies take time, and they soon grow into adult dogs who continue to need time and attention.

Kathy didn't mince words when she described the enormous responsibility of rearing a new puppy. At one point, Kathy paused, but then uttered what turned out to be the most daunting statement of the day. "You know, Kate," she said gently, and with warmth in her smile and eyes, "I know how much you want a puppy, but this might not be the right time for you and your mom to bring a young golden home." Kate responded with a blank stare. I think she believed in her heart that this puppy business was a shoo-in. She was sure she'd get a puppy. Kathy had undoubtedly seen this scenario many times over. "Let's put it this way, Kate, the care and training of a puppy is pretty much a nonstop undertaking, requiring a lot of care for the first year. That's what the puppy needs. It's only fair to the dog that you're able to be home, available, and attentive during this phase of its life."

During the drive home, Kate was a nonstop talking machine—questions, comments, and statements spilled from her. "I can do it, Mom. I can take care of a puppy." Kate addressed the "we" part of the equation, too. She knew I had to be the one to say yes, if she was able to convince me she was not only willing to contribute, but able. When we left the breeder, I'd agreed we had much to consider before we made a final decision. Was it possible we were still not quite ready to take on a dog? I told Kate that it was time for both of us to think and pray about this decision.

The following days were full of talks around our visit to Kathy's kennel. Everything was put on the table, including an honest assessment of how much time a new puppy would spend alone, with me working and Kate in school. The breeder was right about the reasons it might not be the time for a puppy. After much consideration, I knew we needed to wait. Although I knew it was the right decision, I was just as heartbroken as Kate. But she understood, as did I, that the answer was "no, not now." In other words, this wasn't a forever decision, just an assessment that now wasn't the time.

THE PAIN OF SAYING NO

It's important that parents embrace the concept of saying no beyond those toddler years when we hear ourselves saying it so often. However, there are different ways to say no, even nonverbal looks or body language. But the truth is we need to be able to say no when we encounter the more complex situations and reasons that arise as children mature.

We often want to say yes to make our children happy. Sometimes a yes answer will protect them from hurt or save them from a potential failure. But the truth of a situation may reveal itself by the act of saying no, then backing away to observe the consequences even if it results in some short-term pain. This is a difficult part of being an adult. It's not our job to simply make our children happy. We can provide opportunities or say no to potentially detrimental things to protect our children from harm.

Saying no sets a clear boundary, and when done properly it shows we care. If the answer is definitive, then we need to be absolutely sure we mean it. Answers like "I'm not sure yet," or "I'll see," or "probably not," leads to greater frustration and disappointment, and a false sense of hope. Sensing a noncommittal answer, they often turn to whining and begging.

Ginny, an older, wiser mom, babysat Kate when I had a meeting or other commitments. She was a teacher at heart and enjoyed spending time teaching and sharing her wisdom with my two-year-old daughter. When I'd drop Kate off at Ginny's home, Kate was excited to be there because Ginny had planned adventures and learning experiences. Sometimes, Kate grew a bit impatient with our adult conversation and fidgeted or made an untimely request. Ginny then replied or answered to something with an affirmative no. If Kate started to whine, Ginny responded with a singing, jingle type response, "No whining in this house!" Kate clearly understood the directive, and I witnessed the quick change in her disposition. It was on to the next adventure.

Ginny's jingle ended up in my servant mom toolbox as a way to stop whining before it could gather steam. It worked every time.

Single parents have to be especially mindful when saying both yes and no because essentially they are the last word and only have the benefit of one point-of-view. Being confident in saying no was critical to my success as a mom.

Discussing situations is a way to treat your child with respect and to show empathy, which is an essential element for ongoing communication. Without question, though, saying no becomes more challenging as children mature and begin to fight for their independence. However, if you have developed trust and your children believe you have their best interests in mind, it can make the challenge a bit easier.

Your children needn't agree with your answers, but if there is a fact-based approach to your decision, rather than an emotional rant, a need to control, or a decision made from anger and rage, they'll respect you in the long run. Share your reasons for saying no, and do so from the perspective of a parent, not a friend. Not always an easy thing to remember, perhaps, especially for single parents with one child, like Kate and me. Sometimes these relationships can devolve into a kind of roommate scenario. But in my mind this situation made it even more important for me to maintain the mother-child boundary.

Saying no in an affirmative, authoritative way shows that you mean business. Along with that, you follow with an explanation, a reason behind the no. "Because I said so" is *not* a worthy answer.

THE IMPORTANCE OF YES

As our children gather life experiences, it's equally important to say yes as often as possible. I don't mean becoming a pushover, but it's important your children hear affirmative responses. If you hear yourself saying no more often than yes, ask yourself why. Are you tired? Are you insecure about letting go of your child? Is it possible you live with a lot of fear? Valid as your many negative responses may be, they're definitely coming from somewhere. Take some time to dig into why "no" shows up so often.

I heard no too many times as a child, and in looking back, I'm confident they came from a place of fear or insecurity within my mother. Lacking explanations, I never understood the reason for the familiar answer of no. At some point, I stopped asking permission to go places and do things because I knew what the answer would be. A steadfast negative response was imminent, a disappointing predicament for a kid. I even learned what I thought was the best time to ask permission or ask to go somewhere. If it was a brother or sister group request, we would huddle and decide who would approach mom for permission.

"Okay, Mom is sitting down with her tea," my sister would say, looking at me. "You go ask her."

"Me?" I'd respond. "I'm not going to ask her. You ask her."

Round and round we went, even trying to solicit the efforts of my younger brothers. Needless to say, I don't remember a lot of wins on those requests. My heart was laden with too many disappointments, so I was prepared for another no. I was infuriated knowing there was no good reason for the answer.

In any case, part of your child's growth is hearing you say yes to requests, opportunities and adventures. These affirm your child. That's why it's important to explore new situations and gather all the facts children are able to supply based on their age. Allowing kids to try new things is part of their growth, and at times it's part of our growth as parents. Learning when it's appropriate and safe to let them fly on their own is part of the parenting process. I guess we could say that sometimes we also need a push out of our comfort zone.

CHANGES OVER TIME

Three years after saying no to a new puppy Kate and I moved to Petoskey, Michigan. We were still puppy-less but pet parents to our rescue cats, Mat-the-Cat and Rocky. A few months after our arrival, a new acquaintance told us about a litter of golden retriever puppies on the way. She invited us to visit when they arrived. We'd hit another danger zone, but I was ready to start the process again. By this time, Kate had become relentless with the dog begging, but I can't say I blamed her. Time had passed, and we'd reconciled bruised heartstrings after we'd said no to a dog years ago.

I've learned it's sometimes best to sit with a potential decision for a bit and pray about it before making the final decision. A peaceful feeling is the key to knowing I've made a good decision. This time the decision about a dog was one of those I felt good about. It was the right time to welcome a new puppy into our home.

Kate and I accepted our friend's invitation to visit the puppies. We went, we saw, and we conquered the new litter of golden retrievers. We were ready. With puppies running everywhere, Kate picked Carson, or maybe Carson picked her. Both Kate and I were committed to his well-being, his training, and his happiness. He turned out to be the best dog we ever had. (Don't all dog owners say that about their dogs?) He was a great companion to both Kate and me. He followed voice commands, walked off a lead, and was a real charmer. We lived only a few miles from work and school, so we started the day with morning walks, and I headed home at lunch to enjoy a jaunt with Carson. We took him on walks again after school and again after dinner. Playing with a young puppy was good for the soul, and both Kate and I enjoyed this early stage of puppy rearing.

One of my favorite stories about Carson coincided with our move into our new home, just a few blocks away from the quaint downtown gaslight district of Petoskey. I had purchased a mattress from the downtown furniture shop and needed to pay the balance to set up delivery. With the store only three blocks from our home, I suggested Kate take Carson for a walk to pay the balance on the mattress. Kate eagerly took advantage of the chance to share her new puppy.

All in all, the round trip walk to the store should have taken thirty minutes. Then forty minutes passed, and I continued to look down the street to see if Kate and Carson were anywhere in sight. On my final look, I could see the two small figures heading toward me. There Kate was, dragging a very long, broken tree limb behind her. Carson was in her arms rather than following the limb. I was chuckling to myself, anticipating the explanation.

When Kate was within a few feet of our front yard, I shouted, "What happened?"

"Carson was excited walking down to the store," Kate said, "but when we turned around to come home, he walked a few steps and then sat down and wouldn't get up. So I found a big branch in someone's yard and dragged it behind me so he would follow it." Kate was giggling by this time as she described Carson following, but not for long. He got tired and sat on the sidewalk staring at her. "That's why I had to pick him up and carry him the rest of the way home."

Rather than complaining, Kate got a big kick out of the whole trek. I sensed she had a feeling of accomplishment, not to mention love for her new friend. My heart was happy, too. I experienced Kate's display of selflessness, along with her tenacity and problem-solving. She got an A for effort and perseverance, and Carson should have received an A as well. Watching them, I saw quite a sweet picture of companionship, patience, and love at its finest.

YES OR NO, NOT ALWAYS AN EASY CHOICE

The first dog episode was only one example of a complex no answer. Like Kate, I wanted a dog, too, but I had to consider scheduling limitations during the original puppy search. By involving Kate in the question-and-answer process, she had a chance to come to her own realizations about her limitations in sharing pet responsibilities. It was a reality check for me too. That's why I made the decision to say no on our first go-around. But when the opportunity for a puppy presented itself a second time, I was comfortable saying yes and Carson was well worth the wait.

Dogs and other pets teach children several things, perhaps the most obvious is unconditional love. A pet allows a child to embrace this powerful concept, along with acceptance of others, and not just animals. Learning to love and care for a pet teaches lessons that apply elsewhere throughout life. If you've ever loved a pet then you know these lessons never age out. They're permanent. Children also develop a stronger sense of self when they have a pet—dogs are good, but other animals fulfill the same role. Just ask any girl who's ever adored her horse. Many of us shower our cats with love.

Studies back up what we intuitively know, that becoming attached to an animal builds confidence and empathy in adults and children. I believe a pet can help children learn selflessness, which is a deep understanding that everything isn't always all about them. It also drives home the reality that a pet needs care because they can't take care of themselves.

The first decision that delayed bringing a dog into our home later brought Carson into our lives. It ended up as one of the best "not now, but not forever" decisions I ever made. My mom journey has provided countless valuable lessons. Follow your instincts, talk with your child and don't be afraid to say no when it's right and then yes when conditions change.

MOM MEMO
Can We Get a Puppy, Please?

- Knowing when and how to say no is one of the biggest challenges of parenting, but it's also one of the most important.

- It's not the job of servant parents to make their children happy. We can model happiness, but individuals make the decision to be happy.
- Keep your reasons for saying no age appropriate, clear and concise, but firm.
- It's important to say yes to children's requests and support their desire to explore and expand. A yes can be affirming to the child and sends a clear message of trust.
- If you find yourself saying no a lot, examine your reasons.
- If a pet is right for your household, it presents an opportunity for children to learn what it means to take care of another being and shoulder responsibilities that the family shares.
- Caring for a pet is a valuable path to understanding empathy and selflessness, not to mention love.

It takes heart to say no when our heart and brains and guts, and most importantly our pride, are yearning to say yes. Practice.
—Cole Hermonson

SIXTEEN

Overcoming Fear of Failure

Always remember you are braver than you believe. Stronger than you seem, smarter than you think.

—A.A. Milne, from *Winnie the Pooh*

Who doesn't like a challenge? And when put in the proper language and proposed to 12-year-olds, most would probably jump at the chance, especially if a reward is involved. But then again I guess it depends on the challenge itself and of course the ultimate prize.

One beautiful spring day when Kate was about twelve, she came in from school excited, not in a good way, dropping her book bag in the hall with an exasperated and somewhat defeated overall attitude. Curious, I waited to hear what prompted this look of desperation.

After a deep breath she told me the whole story. I listened sympathetically to her heartfelt concern about the impending difficulty. It seemed the entire fourth and fifth grade classes were working towards achieving the Presidential Fitness

Award. The one component of the challenge that caused fear in Kate and many of her classmates was the daunting one-mile run.

Well, honestly, I could understand their anxiety. What 12-year-old jumps out of bed on any given day and decides to run a mile? Training and preparation are minimal in gym class and let's face it, although some kids are born to run, others are in no way built with the physique and energy to run at all—let alone a mile. As a fitness professional, I used to cringe at the thought of forcing everyone, regardless of body type, into one single activity. But there we were, and I could sense the panic in Kate's face and body language.

We found a cozy place to sit and chat. Her feelings were important of course. As a dutiful servant mom, I knew I needed to shut up and just listen. As you could probably guess, I heard recurring themes we can associate with any child: fear of failure, peer pressures and understanding winning versus losing.

Kate explained this run was taking place on their field day, an open event for parents and family to come and cheer their children on. I thought it was a great idea, but Kate didn't agree, because from her perspective, everyone would be watching. "What if I don't finish?" she asked.

"You will finish," I said with encouraging enthusiasm. "How you finish will be up to you. Finish—that's all you need to do. How about we make a plan?"

It was important to me that we talk about possibilities first, and then let Kate choose the most sensible plan. And I knew that with Kate, who's right-brain-oriented (intuitive, big-picture thinkers), we'd need to start at the end and work backwards, creating small checkoff points of accomplishments.

After lightening the drama a bit, we got in the car and drove around our neighborhood. Kate picked the one-mile area that would soon be her training ground, which was the piece she understood. What I understood was that preparation is the essential element that leads to the output of doing our best. Kate had a few weeks before the actual run to train, which gave her a chance to get herself comfortable and visualize the goal of crossing the finish line. Time wasn't a concern, nor was where she placed in the group; just finishing is what the test required. (Kate and I used the SMART goal setting system, which I've described in detail in the Mom Memo section below. You can find it discussed in numerous goal setting books and videos.)

The first task at hand was to walk the mile, so we walked with Carson, our golden retriever. We all simply enjoyed the walk together. Perception is reality. So how far is a mile? We soon learned. Without harping on how far she had walked or what was left, we kept walking until the task was completed. Great job on day one.

Over the course of the next few days and weeks prior to the school field day, Kate bit off one small bite at a time. First a faster walk, then a walk-run. Her eager spirit and natural athleticism swept in, encouraging her to run. She asked questions and put my small tips to good use. Early on she needed to understand breathing, and pacing because if she went too fast at the beginning, she might not have the resources needed to finish.

With a fitness background, I coached and trained clients all the time, but as we all know, family is different. So, I suggested, coached, and cheered Kate on. Every day she was back at it, I was more than enthusiastic and supportive of her efforts. She was literally making fabulous strides.

Then the big ol' bomb drops. Some child in school told my daughter she was fat. Ugh—I despise that word. In my household growing up, we had three things we could never say or call each other: shut up, pig, and fat. My adolescent child was not overweight. (I'm not going to attempt to define size as it relates to a "fat" or "skinny" twelve year old girl.) The point is that in using the word, the other child intended to body shame Kate and undermine her confidence. I wanted to find that child. How dare she? But in listening to my daughter, all that mattered was allowing the hurt and tears to flow. Damage control was next. Kate's self-esteem and confidence were for the moment slightly crushed.

This incident is an example of a type of unacceptable bullying that's unfortunately somewhat common in middle school. Some children attempt to bolster their own self-esteem by working to undermine others. Have you seen the movie "Mean Girls?"

First, I needed to control my own anger and then make a plan. Some mean child hurt Kate's feelings. Where was she? (It could have been a boy, but in this case it was a girl.) Let me at her. Of course, I calmed down. Kids can be mean. From there, it was all about Kate.

My initial step was to comfort and reassure her and listen to what she was feeling and how she wanted to handle the situation. I assured Kate that she was loved for who and what she was. We might not be able to get rid of the bullies but we could prove them wrong by achieving the target goal of running the mile on field day. A healthy, strong body for its own sake is what was at hand. This incident created a hiccup in the training, but Kate also has a fighter's heart, which no one could take that away. I had seen that in her before.

Kate remained faithful to the one mile neighborhood course she set up, from a walk to progressing to the run-walk, and before long, she was running the mile. How fast she ran was not part of the goal—the finish line was her prize.

Field day came and families were cheering all the students on through the various activities. Then it was time for the big event, the one mile run. The fifth-grade classes took their place on the track. Kate was focused, somewhat nervous, but fully committed. Our little pep talk in that morning was all about how doing her best is all that matters. The runners were now in position. The gun sounded. Off they went. Four laps around the track for one mile.

I'm not sure about the runners, but four laps felt like 50 to me. My heart pounded for Kate. After one lap the worry from her face was gone. She was out to capture that finish line. With the entire bleacher section cheering on the group of runners, we couldn't help but experience the positive energy.

Kate ran the four laps and crossed the finish line. Success! That finish line had much more meaning than a simple one-mile run. To this day I have such a clear memory of this entire event. So many emotions ran through my twelve-year-old, and through me as well. First, the race. As a fitness trainer and athlete, I never understood the concept of making everyone do a run regardless of their skill or body composition. Not everyone is a runner.

Next, faced with the challenge, my daughter's feelings were the focus of my attention. I believe in goals, preparation, and tackling the challenge of something you think is impossible. This was a tangible goal.

As for the bullying piece of negatively commenting on the size and weight of another, well I wanted to take care of it myself. But what a great lesson it was in overcoming yet another obstacle, a lesson as a single mom to help direct my daughter through a "now what" scenario.

Confronting bullies, or exposing them, is certainly an option, but it's not always available to us. As a servant mom I took this opportunity to encourage Kate to disregard the negative external stimuli and instead take responsibility for her own success. To keep an eye on her own goals and not bow to someone else's projected opinion of who she was or what she was capable of doing.

In addressing a "weight" comment, it was important to see how my daughter was reacting. Feelings are feelings, they just are. Nothing right or wrong about them. The next piece was to define what matters about the body, which is not about weight, but about health and fitness.

We can and should discuss the power of words with our children. They need help to understand that shaming others for how they look, dress, or act is unkind and unacceptable, and not the way we should define people anyway. Since this kind of criticism or shaming was not tolerated in our home, in no way did I expect Kate to be a recipient of it.

Whether our children expect it or not, it's important that they stand up for themselves and dig deep to stay strong. As servant mothers, it's our job to help kids understand that many derogatory comments and insults come from others based on their own poor self-esteem. We can stress that the work here is to love and honor themselves rather than attempting to fix or berate other people.

Many kids have tried and failed at something and then decided not to try again. They hold back God-given talents and gifts out of fear of failure. Our kids will face battles in their lives just as we have. God didn't say our life would be free of challenges and disappointments. If faith is missing, we may quickly lose our inner peace and fall into fear mode. The committee in our head starts posing "now what?" and "what if?"

If someone wants us to fail, it's certainly not God. The comfort and peace we want to teach our children to reach for comes from God. He has a plan and is leading us to it if we will trust and listen. Fear will attempt to limit us from realizing possibilities, but if we pray when fear pops up, God gives us strength to overcome fear. This is why we need to trust and take a leap of faith, which means we can take steps towards another possibility.

I longed to raise a strong young girl. I prayed every day that life lessons combined with faith, commitment, and unconditional love would create a path for Kate that moved her toward the ability to conquer fear of the unknown. This was to be my gift to her. It allowed me to see her drive and commitment to expanding herself, while also being an example for others. And as always, she continues to teach me as she goes.

Although the fear of failure applies to activities and pursuits of all kinds, physical movement is essential, even critical, to healthy growth and development throughout life. If we help kids move early in life, they'll develop a habit that will serve them well later on. No one needs to argue the benefits of physical movement. But the mental, emotional, social elements are important as well. You'll notice I'm not using the word exercise. There are some bad vibes associated with that word. Perhaps you relate to a bad experience, even way back, associated with "exercise." Perhaps it was being picked last for a team, or dropping the baton in a run, falling in competition. For many people, a negative experience has created a "false start."

Sometimes it's extremely difficult to let go of a bad experience. You don't want your children to come away with the same kind of experience, so watch that you're not projecting your fears onto them. Most important, consider their body types and watch their cognitive or mental state when they engage in an activity. Then wait for it... wait for it... look for the smile.

I've had training in Ayurveda, a holistic approach to healing that originated in India, and have also trained in the Invincible Athlete, a method created by John Doulliard, DC, CAP, a globally recognized leader in natural health, Ayurveda, and Sports

Medicine. Ayurveda emphasizes natural mind-body medicine, balance and in reference to exercise, it means minimal stress to the body during exercise. This method has allowed me to train or work with individuals based on their dosha, a term for basic mind-body types. In essence, this method considers each individual's entire makeup; it's based on Ayurvedic medicine, which holds that health exists when there is a balance of three bodily bio-elements: *Vatta, Pitta, and Kapha.* In combination, these elements define your *dosha.* (If you're interested in learning more about Ayurvedic medicine and the three body types, see the resources listed in the back of this book and on my website.)

Regardless of what approach to health you subscribe to, you probably agree that mental and physical makeup varies widely among individuals, including our children. However, you can put aside preconceived ideas about what activity you'd like to see your kids do well, perhaps one in which you excelled, or wished you had. If you take a "wannabe" approach, though, you run the risk of overlooking or diminishing what a particular child's gift—and special strengths—might be in another area you hadn't even considered.

Who doesn't want to set their children up for success? It's difficult if not impossible to mold others, including our kids, into what we want them to be. Instead, helping them develop their natural talents and ability, guiding them to be the best version of themselves, or as the saying goes, all they can be. This is the essence of being a servant mom, servant parent, or servant leader in general.

MOM MEMO
Overcoming Fear of Failure

- Help expose and direct your children to try a variety of activities so you can learn what draws in their attention and enthusiasm while expressing their gifts and talents.
- Help your child understand the importance of setting goals. The SMART system is one well-known goal setting method, although there are many to choose from. The principles of the SMART method are:

Specific—I want to run vs. I want to run a mile
Measurable—the goal is trackable, meaningful
Attainable—a mile is doable with the goal to focus on finishing, not my time
Realistic—I can run a mile as a new runner, not a five mile run
Timely—time sensitive. I can prepare for this for a month and then run a mile

- Many forces work against our kids and threaten to cast a blanket of fear over them. Embrace overcoming fear of failure by encouraging your kids to build a relationship in God.
- Teach trust and leaning into God. He didn't create us to live in fear.

So do not fear, for I am with you; do not be dismayed, for I am your God. I will strengthen you and help you; I will uphold you with my righteous right hand.
—Isaiah 41: 8-10

SEVENTEEN

Who's Coming Over Tonight?

Be our guest whether you come in to visit, or just to rest, when you enter our home may you be blessed.

—Unknown

Growing up, I had a reoccurring story playing in my head. Whether I was riding my bike, taking a walk, or looking out the window from the back seat of the family car, I'd study the houses as I passed by. I'd glance at the yard, gaze at the front door, then think beyond the door and into the house. I visualized a happy family laughing, having fun, and perhaps enjoying a house full of guests. That's what I pictured going on beyond the white picket fence. Whether this was a fairytale-life or not, I wanted in on it. I longed for laughter, a tension-free environment and an open-door policy that extended last-minute invitations to friends or family who would always be welcome to come over to our house. Instead I was resentful because I thought others made this happen easily, even routinely. But in my house, having people visit involved a kind of struggle and stress. An event like this usually had to be planned way ahead of time. I wanted something different, namely a home that welcomed friends, family, and even strangers at virtually any time with open arms.

Creating a comfortable space we call home is important for kids. They need a stable, safe environment that supports their overall well-being, even while acknowledging that no home is always stress-free. In fact, stress is normal, universal, and healthy for children, too, because coping with the ordinary stresses of life helps build emotional strength and resilience. But too much stress, especially ongoing and unrelenting stress, is detrimental, which is why I advise parents to do the best they can to resolve or at least limit stressful situations.

I'm aware that this isn't an easy job. Millions of families struggle to find ways to handle the normal stresses of life, not to mention the pressures added by the recent pandemic. However, a home filled with unspecified anxiety and continued uncertainty creates chronic stress, which may be beyond a child's ability to comprehend or handle. At times, a child might perceive a situation as even worse than it is. This is why it's important that you help your children understand that adult life has certain challenges. Using age-appropriate language, you can tell your children that although you're a bit stressed, you're doing your best to manage the situation. You can reassure them that the issue isn't something they need to be concerned about.

As I went through counseling and began to work with more healing modalities and energy work, I tapped into what it felt like to be under so much stress as a young kid. Becoming aware of those feelings strengthened my resolve to do everything in my power as a new mom to deal with that childhood baggage, all of it. That would allow me to move to a place of confidence and conviction about being a healthy, work-in-process servant mom.

From the time Kate was born, I was adamant about honoring one of my commitments to her and myself. I'd create a home full of love and laughter. To accomplish this I established a set of values and boundaries that facilitated an environment defined by unconditional love, which extended to anyone who came into our home. Doing my best to keep tension out of our home was critical in my attempt to raise a self-confident and secure child, which is why rules and expectations existed. They were conveyed and defined through clear communication—no guessing games or confusing gray areas in the house rules and responsibilities.

IT'S CALLED HOSPITALITY

As a servant mom, my open-door policy was extremely important and was the way I embraced and lived out the concept of "hospitality." What does hospitality mean and why the call to take this to heart? How could Kate and I extend hospitality and be an example to others? Hospitality can mean something as simple as inviting people over for dinner or to a backyard picnic.

I worked in the hospitality industry for many years, specifically, the spa business, in which our job was defined by anticipating the needs of others, our customers. Our constant theme was "the customer comes first." The message of this mantra was to welcome the guest and create a home-away-from-home atmosphere. When training work teams, I'd ask if the desire to serve is innate or trainable. Over 80% of my work teams believed the desire is innate. That means that most people, at least in the hospitality business, believe that we as humans have a natural inclination to be hospitable towards others. But it's also possible these individuals had learned to feel this way, perhaps at home. Maybe that's what inspired them to seek this type of work. In either case, authentic hospitality comes from the heart, and it comes more naturally to some individuals than to others.

For families rooted in ~~a~~ faith, hospitality means welcoming people into our lives, reaching out to anyone in need of solace or temporary comfort. As individuals of faith, we're called to this ministry in one form or another, including the idea of making our house a home, ultimately an extension of who we are. This also means extending a kind word to those we meet, friend or stranger. It also means paying attention to those who cross your path and taking time to do more than recognize, but to also engage. Showing interest and true regard for another is the essence of being hospitable. Through our hospitality we can affect the lives of others in a very personal way.

Part of my motivation to create a hospitable space came from my desire to have our house be a hangout, a safe haven for Kate and her friends. I welcomed any kid that wanted to spend time there. If kids needed a place to go, they could land with us and I established rules around what that invitation would look like. Through Kate's middle-school years I set clear boundaries and rules about who she could have in in our home and when, the first rule being that I had to be present. With that boundary in place, our door was open to her friends for years. During high school, the rules changed as she matured and took on more responsibility, but she agreed to communicate with me about who would come over and when. Still, I minimized the time she'd be alone in the house with friends.

During her middle school years, Kate's involvement in sports and extracurricular activities kept her at school until close to five o'clock each night. I'd generally pick her up at her school on the way home from work. If she walked home from school, she'd let herself in, take our dog out, and then lock the door behind her.

When Kate was in middle school, I got a call from her at work. My heart skipped a beat as I hoped we weren't having an emergency. She got to the point quickly. "Um, Tracy is here with me. Her mom is going to be really late to come get her after practice. I didn't want her waiting there by herself, so I invited her back here. I know the rule about you needing to be home but I didn't want to leave her alone." She rattled off the things she was supposed to do once she got home and said they were done. Now they were just sitting around.

I smiled inside sensing Kate wanted to know that she wasn't in trouble, but had actually done the right thing. "Well that's nice that you invited Tracy to the house," I replied. "It was the right thing to do."

Kate then filled in the details to confirm that she was honoring the "no company when Mom's not home" rule. I saw this as proving she could handle an exception to the rule. Rules need to bend at times, and as parents we can see our children taking responsibility and maturely making a decision, which expands the spirit of the rule, not just the rote words of it. I commended Kate on her thoughtfulness and told her to share a snack with Tracy, adding that I'd be home in about 15 minutes.

I showed my approval of what Kate did in words, but also through my body language when I arrived home and greeted them. I had no hidden disapproval agenda because Kate wasn't in trouble. I was proud of her decision and let her know it.

Kate's next question came quickly—even before I got my coat off. "Can Tracy stay for dinner?"

I enjoyed Kate's easy spontaneity, knowing it wasn't about the menu, but the company and comfort of having someone in our home. I was happy Kate was living out what she didn't even realize at that time was the gift of being hospitable. Children don't use that word because they want the company, the experience of hanging out with a friend, especially if they're an only child like Kate. As I said, this showed Kate's ability to be spontaneous and comfortable in making a request and getting an honest answer. Of course, the possibility existed that it wouldn't have worked for me, perhaps because I wasn't either prepared for company or had other plans for the that particular evening. However, in those cases, I offered a raincheck, and later we'd set a date and follow through.

FAMILIES OF CHOICE

Hospitality extended beyond casual friends and acquaintances, and still does. For one thing, our extended family lives a few states away, so like many people do today, we created a "family of choice." This happened rather unconsciously wherever we lived. We opened the door, literally, and love and hospitality grew in our home with new found friends that were soon like family. We hosted holidays, birthday parties, or impromptu Sunday coffee at our house after church.

One of my favorite hospitality endeavors took place one Halloween evening in Petoskey, Michigan. Kate was ready for the day with her costume and a plan in mind. Being an eighth grader, trick or treating was all about convening with friends and conquering a neighborhood for Halloween treats. We lived in Petoskey's historic downtown neighborhood and it was *the* place to trick or treat. Families parked their cars close by in parking lots and then walked up and down these streets to trick or treat. Houses were close together, a big win in terms of loading a trick or treat bag with goodies. Being in the center of town, Kate asked if she could have a few friends over to go trick or treating with her.

I was okay with that and offered a plan. "How about you come here after volleyball and we'll order pizza. Then you can all leave from here."

We first created a small get together, but it slowly morphed into a party with a few more guests. That was okay. I was all in and happy we would be the landing pad for this group of young teenagers. I'd made it my business to know Kate's friends, something I highly recommend, so I was familiar with the kids who'd be coming to the house. Her friends respected me and I appreciated each one as an individual.

What a memorable Halloween it turned out to be. Kate and her friends walked to the house after school and we ordered the pizza as planned. I recall the house being filled with laughter as the kids entertained each other. Just the way I had imagined so many years ago when driving with my parents. By the way, I'm half Italian, so true to the stereotype, food is ever plentiful, enough to go around, and then some. I'm happy with a full house—the more the merrier is my motto. After pizza, they got into their costume mode, which included makeup and more, and were soon ready to go out. Everyone was up for some fun and their mission to tackle the neighborhood. I set the guidelines, including the curfew, and out the door they went.

It was an unusually warm night for Halloween in Northern Michigan, which are often chilly affairs, an advantage for me as I sat on the porch handing out candy. I got a chance to admire the creative costumes of the hundreds of kids that stopped at our home that evening. I was so grateful that our home was a place that Kate wanted as the evening hangout for her and her friends.

Another time we estimated that over 200 kids came to our house for Halloween. Partway through the festivities, I left the porch and went in the house to grab more candy to add to the huge candy bowl on the porch. As I walked back to the front door I heard voices, and within seconds I saw three boys running down the sidewalk. They had taken the entire bowl of candy and emptied it into their pillowcases. I put the candy down, grabbed the bowl and ran like hell after them. I caught up to them and was out of breath, but I managed to say, "Put the candy back in this bowl."

They looked at me, but didn't act. Finally, I said, "You see all these police officers patrolling the area? Don't tempt me to walk over there and introduce you to them." With dignity and assertiveness I asked them to return the candy so other kids could receive something from our house. They quickly reached into their sacks and filled our empty bowl back up. Whether it was the original candy or not the goods were returned.

Kids, like parents, are bound to learn that some people will take advantage of other people's hospitality. These "candy thieves" demonstrate that learning how to accept hospitality is as important as extending it. It also shows that being hospitable or understanding what it means doesn't come naturally to everyone. On occasion, however, it can be a teachable moment.

A PLACE WE WANT TO BE

Hospitality creates a home where kids want to be because it's welcoming and familiar. Although they'll never admit it, kids need—even crave—adult role models. I wasn't shy about posing questions to Kate's friends and listening to their responses, which gave me an opportunity to show my interest in them and hear more of their thoughts. We moved five times when Kate was growing up, and never had a big house or extra rooms, but that didn't stop us from having what I'd always wanted, a welcoming home.

At the same time, as a servant mom, I maintained structure in our home, and I demanded respect and received it. I returned it in kind to any child I encountered, inside or outside our home. In other words, we treated others as we wanted to be treated, a principle accepted by all the kids who came in and out of our house. It was a blessing to be an adult in a position to offer hospitality to other kids. I realize not everyone can create this atmosphere the same way I did, with amenities like warm homemade cookies and room for sleepovers—and the unforgettable giggling that those occasions invariably bring. But there are many ways to be welcoming to others.

Some parents even have the privilege of being safe haven or less stressful space for kids in the midst of small or large crises. One of Kate's friends was going through the heartache of being away from her mom, who was suffering from a brain tumor. We could open a space for her that ultimately made a difference in her life, even if that wasn't fully understood until many years had passed. Good times or tough times, our door was open.

HOSPITALITY TO THOSE WE DON'T KNOW

Our involvement in church outreach was another way of understanding the meaning of hospitality beyond the organized parish service projects. When Kate was in high school, we began to sponsor Frandi, a five-year-old boy who lives in the Dominican Republic. We did this through our church and a Christian based organization. Sponsorship meant making a monthly donation, but we also had opportunities to write letters and share pictures. Kate was a part of this until she left for college, and Frandi is still my sponsored child today and is now preparing to head to college. I continue to share updates and pictures with Kate. So, this particular hospitality is about kindness and serving both friends and those who are ultimately strangers. Integrating a particular cause or charity into your family life is a way to model a spiritual practice and habit that can last a lifetime. For one thing, it can be an example of giving for its own sake, without expecting to receive anything in return. Generosity to others is a form of hospitality that produces a plethora of intangible gifts.

Hospitality generally starts inside our homes, the safe place we create that cherishes and respects family time and nurtures a welcoming sociable atmosphere. This means opening a door in our hearts and in our busy lives in order to serve others. It pleased me to know Kate understood and embraced this. She grew up understanding that our special space was available for a friend and that our kitchen was a place to make a meal for an acquaintance in need.

For me, the key was spontaneity, something I focused on learning before Kate was born. My childhood home was highly structured, so last minute requests were almost always met with a fast "no." In my adult life, I changed that with specific intention. I accepted last minute invitations and extended them, too. Being single, I was free to create the environment and make the decisions. When a request or last minute invitation came up, it was up to me and only me to say yes or no.

I also created the feeling or tone in the house, which meant not concerning myself with what the house looked like before inviting someone over. I didn't put pressure on myself to fix an elaborate meal. Guests don't care if you're a great cook or have the expensive place settings with matching napkins, or the other trappings of entertainment touted on Food Network or HGTV. Hospitality is about relationships and sharing time. These events were joint, cooperative efforts Kate helped with everything from cooking to cleanup. We made each step fun. Good thing, because little did I know how memorable and formative those years and times would be.

Putting together these shared meals and opening our door to our guests led to Kate's frequent question, repeated from the time she was a young child and beyond: "Who's coming over tonight?" Or, she might say, "Can we invite someone over tonight?" She wanted to create a good time and was always happy when entertaining friends, hers or mine. It didn't matter. Now as an adult she has a gift for making others feel comfortable and welcome in her home.

YOUR OWN BRAND OF HOSPITALITY

Not everyone has either the desire or the resources to have social events, or even guests for dinner. Everyone understands that. However, you can exercise hospitality in many ways by simply asking yourself how you can make others feel special. For people of faith, hospitality can mean something different from socializing in our homes. It can be defined as a spiritual gift designed to enrich the lives of others through our outreach. We've defined hospitality in more than one way in our family of two—and so have many others. Dropping off a prepared or purchased meal to someone or delivering groceries to a family or individual dealing with loss or illness is certainly a show of hospitality. During the recent pandemic, picking up items for neighbors and friends was a great service in the spirit of hospitality. Perhaps you volunteered to organize a family get-together that wouldn't have happen if you hadn't made the effort. The location doesn't matter, but your open heart combined with the additional effort and time spent fits the definition of hospitality.

I began this chapter by talking about stress. Opening our hearts, sharing what little we might have, and looking out for the needs of others can provide a feeling of abundance that can relieve our stress. By helping others, we feel less helpless ourselves.

Your actions build and nourish a hospitable heart in your children. By watching you, they learn the rhythms of giving and receiving, which is an integral piece of their development. It can be easy to stay in a world of "me." Being distracted and busy is a common theme today, but by definition hospitality pushes beyond our own life and family to embrace others. It's habitual to say, "Family comes first," and most everyone lives with that as a motto of sorts, but the cliché begs the question, "How can I love my neighbor?"

MOM MEMO
Who's Coming Over Tonight?

- Your children learn to be hospitable to those they know and those they don't by watching you, so include them in creating a welcoming atmosphere in your home—a priceless gift.
- Be yourself, and make your own rules for your dinner table, with or without guests—make it time for laughter and storytelling. Tell your kids and their guests that cellphones aren't invited to come to the dinner table.
- Find a cause or charity that allows your children to open their hearts and give of themselves without expectation. Learning to share their home, their talents, even their joyful spirits are priceless acts.
- Explain that opportunities to extend hospitality show up often, but we may not immediately understand the full meaning of the action, but the insights will show up later—maybe even years later.

Keep on loving one another as brothers and sisters. Do not forget to show hospitality to strangers, for by so doing some people have shown hospitality to angels without knowing it.
—Hebrews 13:1-2

EIGHTEEN

On Stage

Be yourself, everybody else is taken....

—Oscar Wilde

For many of us, entering a theater is stepping into a magical space that fills us with wonder. Our bodies tingle as our creativity is triggered by the sense of possibilities. Theater, dance, musicals, and choirs of any kind have been constants throughout my life, and no less so when I became a mom. Luckily, Kate developed the love of both performance and performing.

Kate played piano and flute and sang in the choir, which led to participating in several musical productions. From an early age, weekly dance lessons were on Kate's afterschool docket. Those early days of pink tutus and recitals remain precious memories because Kate loved ballet and jazz, but tap dance was her favorite. Intuitively, most parents of childhood dancers, musicians, and other on-stage performers understand that children gain experience well beyond the skills of the art. They learn to overcome nervousness and how to collaborate with others. Kate's ability to being part of a team of dancers taught her life lessons that extended far beyond the choreography and production.

One of the highlights of my week was picking Kate up from dance class after work. Although the studio's policy barred parents from watching their children in class, we caught sneak peeks now and again. The commute from work to the studio was tight, so Kate's instructor assured me it was okay if I happened to be a few minutes late picking her up. She'd let Kate tap with the adult tap class that started right after Kate's. I'd walk in to find her tapping away with the adults, enjoying herself and keeping up so well that her teacher communicated ways for me to not show up on time.

My uncle gave me a piano that I set against one wall in our living room. I enjoyed playing, and music routinely filled our home. Kate soon took to the piano, so lessons became another part of her after-school schedule.

Most children don't need much coaxing when it comes to participating in activities. If they are sociable types it's a chance to meet new people and develop new skills. Kate learned early on that preparing for recitals and concerts meant memorizing material and committing to regular practice and rehearsals, which she was usually up for. Meanwhile, school and other activities also bring demands, so kids quickly discover that a busy schedule isn't always fun. They also learn that taking on challenging activities can lead to disappointments and awkward moments. Demanding teachers and directors created high expectations for their young apprentices, which in turn created opportunities for some important life lessons for Kate.

THE PIANO "LESSON"

Kate's piano teacher in middle school, Mrs. Z gave lessons in her home, conveniently located only a few blocks from our house. Mrs. Z had high expectations for all her students, and Kate was no exception. She stuck to her practice time and worked hard to master the piano. Kate was likely a bit intimidated by Mrs. Z, with her tight ponytail and perpetually scowling expression. No two ways about it, this teacher meant business. Work hard and play hard on that piano.

The annual piano recital was held each spring. One particular recital is emblazoned in Kate's mind. She still brings up *that* recital and laughs about it, at the same time she "jokes" about the experience giving her PTSD—post-traumatic stress disorder. Mrs. Z chose music selections for each student, and every day I heard Kate practicing one of her two pieces. Let's just say she was less than enthusiastic about the selection. One spot in the piece created a hurdle, and during practices, Kate would hit the wrong note but make the correction and move on. However, when this bump in the musical road happened during a lesson with Mrs. Z, the energy was different. Mrs. Z stood behind her, correcting the error, and directing Kate to play that part again, which delivered a subconscious message of, *"Right there...this is where you mess up."*

These practices ruffled Kate's feathers and increased her frustration. She'd come home from a lesson resentful of Mrs. Z and annoyed at herself. It was a lesson for both of us on so many levels, including the need for persistent practice, patience, understanding, as well as adapting to teaching styles, and learning how to coach through a hurdle. In the process, I provided encouragement, but I also put a different spin on the challenge, such as Kate visualizing herself playing the right note. And how about lifting some of that self-induced pressure?

Recital day finally came and we headed to the venue, where Kate joined her teacher and the other students while I headed to my seat. When Kate's turn came, she took her place at the piano and began—so beautifully. With all the practicing at home, I'd committed this piece to memory, so I knew it was only a matter of time until she got to "the spot." It was coming, that note that gave her so much grief. As she started the measure, my heart raced. Naturally, I wanted this to go as smooth as silk. The measure quickly approached with a gentle slow down and then *plunk*. My heart sank. She'd hit the wrong key, and no matter how quickly she corrected herself there was no denying the mistake. Kate finished the piece with finesse. Rising from the piano bench, she mustered a half-smile and took a bow before scurrying off the stage.

Oh boy, what would our post-recital conversation be like?

When I saw her after the recital, I gave her a hug, but didn't start talking about what happened, or, as we parents sometimes do, talk away all the troubles, as if we can wipe the slate clean. With a few tears and a slight sense of defeat, Kate opened up later that evening. She was tough on herself, simultaneously irritated and dismayed. Internally, my emotions came up in rapid fire fashion, although I certainly didn't tell Kate I was mad at myself or mad at the teacher, neither of which were rational responses. I was embarrassed for her, of course, but I didn't hover or try to fix the situation with a lot of empty talk. In these situations, it's important that we allow kids to feel what they need to feel in the moment.

At some point I asked Kate what she did *well* in the recital piece and she recognized she had plenty to highlight. This opened a conversation about chasing perfection and moved into affirming how far she'd come with her lessons and performances. One of the things that performance at all levels teaches is the protocol that we start and finish no matter what happens.

When kids—and adults—watch figure skaters compete, we always note that when they fall on a jump they quickly get up and pick up the program. The audience often applauds skaters as they get back to the rhythm of their performance. That's what Kate had already learned about performance. She hit a glitch and moved on. She didn't quit and walk off the stage.

AVOIDING THE PERFECTION TRAP

At any age, the quest for perfection is a vicious cycle, and it never stops because no one wins. What matters for parents and kids is to strive to do our best. Even the most well-prepared athletes, artists, and performers experience performance hiccups. Look at what happens during the Olympics. Like clockwork, a tiny slip-up costs an athlete a medal. Pursuing perfection creates pressure that taunts and teases.

Parents (and other adults involved in their lives) need to help kids internalize Winston Churchill's famous words, *Perfectionism is the enemy of progress.* This quote carries a lot of meaning today because young people appear to strive for perfection. I talk to young parents, in my role as youth minister and mentor, who tell me their children experience intense stress and anxiety. Many parents believe this strain is self-imposed. However, we can't take ourselves out of the equation, because often our children's stress and anxiety originates from our expectations of them. The kids believe this comes from their parents and others. We need to listen because we might unknowingly fan the flames of perfectionism. Without being aware of it, we could be reinforcing their self-imposed high standards and their harsh self-criticism if they don't quite reach the top.

Personal expectations and peer pressure combine to form the dilemma. I've had parents talk about their kids' internal pressure for self-acceptance, while at the same time they seek acceptance in their peer world. Social media doesn't help these days. Frankly, I'm grateful social media with all its pitfalls was not a part of life when Kate was young. I rarely meet parents of adult kids who don't agree.

ALL THE WORLD'S A STAGE

By William Shakespeare (from *As You Like It*)

All the world's a stage,
And all the men and women merely players;
They have their exits and their entrances;
And one man in his time plays many parts,

LIFELONG LESSONS

Kate's disappointment in her performance turned out to be valuable for her and for me. I had practice in treading through a minefield of emotions as I tried to be there for Kate. I couldn't fix anything. All I could do was help her come to terms with her glitch. As I said, Kate now jokes about her PTSD over her "plucked note" and Mrs. Z.

Sometimes the best-laid performance plans just don't work out. For example, over time Kate tired of Mrs. Z's teaching style and sadly her joy and enthusiasm for the instrument went out the window. Although I am a fan of hard work and discipline, Kate and this teacher weren't compatible. But I missed an opportunity to provide a remedy for that. If I had to do it over again, I'd have found another teacher for Kate and perhaps her interest would have lasted longer. She also had begun to play the flute and that remained an interest well into high school.

Guiding our kids to put mistakes and embarrassing moments in perspective is important for most everything they'll do in the future. Most of the time, they'll find other opportunities to have successes. In Kate's case, she had a lead role in a musical in middle school, and she performed with her show choir, along with delivering speeches.

What these stages provided for her and virtually all kids were one valuable opportunity after another. Think of how intimidating a literal stage can be. It's usually raised four feet or so above ground level, props are in place, bright lights highlight the scene, and when the performance starts, hundreds of pairs of eyes are staring at the performers. Performing can teach children and teens how to manage the bubbly excitement mixed with some nervousness and fear. As parents, we pray that our children can and will share their gifts out in the world. We want them to show up well-prepared to deliver the best possible performance they can.

Years ago, I had a company I named Backdrop Productions, which is also where ROUTEEN developed (see chapter 11), a performance group that impacted the lives of teens and adults. As I struggled to name my company I thought about how much work goes into creating the backdrops that sets the atmosphere of theatrical performances, which in turn produce the temperament, the feeling tone, around each scene. I think of this as analogous to what parents attempt to do. We hope to create a strong backdrop that prepares our children for their performance in their world.

Through schools, community centers, and faith groups, our children usually find opportunities to practice for the bigger life stage, no matter what role they decide to play. Performance on life's stages is about more than simply showing up. We bring our previous experiences and earlier lessons learned as we share our skills and gifts, which is how we influence and inspire each other every day. With our children, we can witness that what they take with them as they mature helps them inspire those around them, not with their solo performances, but by the people they have become. In other words, if kids show up for "opening night," however it's defined for your child's activity, they'll be motivated to show up for the metaphorical opening nights that are part of fulfilling their purpose throughout life.

THE PITCHER NEEDS A CATCHER

Many childhood activities, like the theater, require a group or a team. These are priceless opportunities for kids to develop social skills and practice the give and take of cooperation. This is where they gain an appreciation of what it means to work together to raise the curtain or make it to the final inning, win or lose. Truly understanding that no one finds success as an island is one of the most important life lessons our kids can learn from participating in all kinds of arts, athletics, and academic programs that require teamwork.

We also need each other as we develop resiliency, the ability to learn from hiccups and losses. After you've coached your children to put their best effort forward, you hope to hear an enthusiastic "I did it!" If not, then you'll shout, "You did it!" Maybe the "performance," whatever it was, hit a personal best, or perhaps it hit a wrong note somewhere or other mistakes changed the outcome. But, *resiliency* means handling disappointments and showing up again. Win or lose, we parents can provide the standing ovation.

THE POWER OF A SINGLE STAGE

The act of being on a real stage, even if only once, can change kids' lives. I have experienced it, and I've seen it in action. Sporting events, chorus or band, science fairs, musical performances, dance recitals, debates, class presentations, and delivering a speech all include elements of stage presence. So if your children choose an activity, commit to the work, and follow through with the performance—even once—they will come away with greater self-confidence and strength of character. Our mom and dad enthusiasm can't guarantee anything except encouragement that helps boost our kids' confidence. Show up for your children, and they'll always know you're their biggest fan.

The process starts when children show enough interest in an activity over time that we can suggest and encourage them to commit to a goal around it, whatever form the performance takes. Sometimes we need to take time to coax kids a little and emphasize that we believe in their capabilities, but that's okay, because this is how we watch the exciting transformation from "I can't" to "I've got this."

Don't let economic limitations stop you from encouraging participation. Many programs in the schools are free or have only a low fee, so start with arts and sports programs at your child's school. Take advantage of church or community resources to find more opportunities. Many kids enjoy their first chance to play a musical instrument, participate in dance, give presentations or speeches, or play a sport because of school programs and community centers like the YWCA-YMCA, The Boys & Girls Club, and so forth.

If challenges and hiccups show up, use them as your chance to talk about resilience and how we learn from mishaps on our journeys. It's a cliché, but the best guideline of all is that there are no failures, but only lessons learned. We can all name a plethora of famous historical figures and contemporary individuals who tell stories of major losses and defeat before successfully reaching their goals.

HANDLING THE GLITCHES

Sometimes kids balk at a particular goal because they don't own it, the parents do. In other words, the parents and kids don't share the same vision of success. Parents can get stuck in their own desires, thus coaxing children in the wrong direction. This can cause a push-pull relationship that sometimes lasts a lifetime. It's a cliché, but we've all heard about the dad who envisions a young athlete and can't accept that the science club is a better fit for his child. You might have fantasized about a musical child, but your child would rather play on the volleyball team at the community center. Of course it's possible, the same child can do both things, but in any case, our job is to tap into what draws our children's interest, which may be much different from ours.

No matter what our kids commit to, the journey will have some ups and downs. Our kids will forget their lines, drop a prop, miss a perfect score or grade on a test, but if they've been encouraged to do their best and leave perfectionism out of the equation, most kids will find value in the experience and move on. If they're disappointed, then so be it. Sometimes they're disappointed in themselves because they know they didn't prepare well enough. That's a lesson in itself. They can resolve to do better next time.

Children need to experience defeats and minor blows to grasp their limits, of course, but also to develop resiliency. Uncomfortable news, disappointments, and falling short of expectations are all a part of life, but so is the acceptance that life isn't about being perfect.

Resiliency is about accepting mistakes, disappointments, and losses, extracting the lessons learned and moving on. When appropriate, be transparent about your own mistakes and small non-successes. We can teach our kids by example that an essential part of life is getting through defeats, awkward moments, disappointments, and heartache. As servant leaders we don't ignore the upset, but rather, guide them in solving the problem, accepting the outcome, and putting the loss or disappointment in perspective. As hard as it is to accept sometimes, it's not our job to fix these kinds of life events.

As parents, we often see these lessons in resiliency coming, and it can be painful to watch, but the kids learn more easily in the long run if parents stay out of the way and allow the process to take place. If we try to fix "teaching moments," the bigger picture, the more significant growth opportunity will be missed. This is painful at times, but our hands-off attitude is what's necessary to raise a strong, resilient child who can handle life's performances. In the so-called real world, our grown children will perform in some way to deliver their unique message under a metaphorical spotlight. It may be for themselves, for an audience of one, or for a crowd of thousands—who knows?

MOM MEMO
On Stage

- You're preparing your children for the life stage. Activities that seem ordinary or simple like a pickup basketball game or entering a science or art fair can provide a stage to learn significant life lessons.
- Being on stage, literally, even once, can be a life-changing, confidence-building event. Help your child find the activities that provide a venue for commitment, effort, and performance.
- Don't assume you can't afford an activity—cast a wide net to find activities that match your child's interests. You might be surprised by the number of opportunities available that fit your budget.

- Be prepared to show up to support your children's efforts, and depending on the stage, show up for the actual performance, too. You will always be your child's biggest fan.
- Keep in mind that you're preparing your children for "onstage" moments in life by what you create and provide for them "off stage."

On the stage of life, characters come and go after their performance. If someone is gone – just smile and clap in appreciation for them, for what good they did and what lessons they taught.

—Anonymous

NINETEEN

Thinking of You

Between a million yesterdays and a million tomorrows, there's only one today. And I would never let it pass without telling you I'm thinking of you.

—Mitch Cuento, Author

There's nothing like receiving a handwritten note. Whether it comes in the mail, is left on your desk, or perhaps tucked away in your backpack or suitcase, a simple gesture lets you know that someone is thinking of you. For years now I've saved notes and letters from family or friends, or from students or employees, and, of course, those from my daughter. I've tucked away quite a few notes from loved ones in dresser drawers. In some cases, the paper is tattered and worn and the handwriting difficult to read because the ink has faded over time. Somehow, that doesn't matter, because the message is clear enough to bring a smile to my face without fail.

Now and again I'll read through these unique keepsakes, and I mentally travel back to the memory associated with the note I'm holding my hand. Each carries a treasured memory and a reminder of the effort behind this simple act of love. I've kept a few store-bought cards with sweet notes written in them or letters folded inside, but it's usually the small, homemade notes that have the most significant and lasting impact. Two of my favorites are worn sticky notes and a small cut-out heart with a single-word message.

When looking at my collection of notes, I'm immediately connected to the original reason for the note or letter, and those memories can be overwhelming. Some aren't associated with any occasion or event, but were randomly sent or left behind for me to find. As a servant mom, it's a reminder of the ways I've used handwritten notes to express love and admiration to many people, but specifically to my daughter. Starting this practice with Kate also meant having the pleasure of watching it turn into a practice for her.

The content of these saved notes always meant something to me at the time, which prompted me to keep them; sometimes I turned a note or card into a bookmark or a placeholder in my Bible. Even if I put it in a corner of a drawer, the note itself told me that the person was thinking of me, often many years ago now. Their age now doesn't matter because those notes had always arrived at the perfect time.

I'm not the first to say that the handwritten note is becoming rarer by the day. Cell phones make it so easy to send a quick text. A three word "I love you," a cartoon animal with outstretched arms and a big "Hello." Or, maybe you get a single emoji or a long line of them. Fair enough, this is communication, but I'm still a fan of a handwritten note. At one time a hint of mystery could surround a loved one's note written on a matchbook cover, or the back of receipt, or even a paper napkin from a restaurant. A note could appear inside a book—not so easy on a digital download. It gave immediacy to the quick note, as if the person was compelled to grab whatever was handy in the moment to get the thought down. Often it was enough to simply say, "Wanted to let you know I was thinking of you." Notes like these could be left on a windshield of a car or even inside the refrigerator—or a packed suitcase. That's the same way we can share our thoughts and feelings for our children even today, no phone required.

MESSAGES STICK...FOR YEARS

Growing up, my mother would randomly leave notes in our lunch boxes. We didn't know when they might appear, and I recall looking forward to seeing her "I love you," there in writing. I knew deep inside my mom loved me, but I admit to wondering about that at times. I saved those notes from my lunchbox, and when I had doubts or insecurities I'd read these keepsakes in the privacy of my bedroom. Obviously, they had significance for me because decades later, I'm writing about them.

As a junior in high school, I attended a weekend retreat for teens, where we shared a powerful experience called "joy power." Each retreatant received a large mailing envelope filled with a personalized letter from each retreat team member. The envelope also contained letters from Mom and Dad. We gathered in a large room with music playing amidst the noise of envelopes being torn open and paper unfolded. We each sat quietly and read our notes, a touching interlude for many, including me. For most teens today, reading a letter from their parents is a unique experience to begin with.

Parents had been instructed to express in writing their sentiments and deep feelings for their children. Apparently, they did just that and emotions filled that room. I was no exception. I had a letter from both my mom and my dad. Even all these years later, it's hard for me to express how deeply touched and grateful I was for these letters. I still have them, of course, but after being opened, unfolded, read, and refolded, they're fragile now, like tissue paper. No matter, their words helped me through challenging times when I needed reassurance that I was loved as a daughter and a mature young woman in my own right.

MY MOM-NOTES

Having become a note writer myself, I've derived great pleasure from sending notes to people for various reasons. That carried into my days as a mother. As I've said before, I had two essential missions as a mom: I wanted to make sure Kate never doubted how much she was loved, and second, I intended to make our home a respite full of love and laughter. So in fulfilling the first and most important mission, I used notes to communicate with Kate. Typically, I employed the element of surprise. That meant using sticky notes, cards, and random creative materials to convey a thought, congratulations, thinking of you, or my favorite, the unexpected "just because" message. I didn't need a reason to say whatever was on my mind.

After our divorce, Kate's dad and I lived in separate states, so regular weekly dinners or weekends with her dad were impossible. Instead, Kate went on more extended trips to see her dad and his new family, sometimes lasting six-weeks. Kate's father and I were on excellent terms, and I was committed to keeping things healthy and amicable between us. Kate's best interest was all that mattered. That theme continued throughout Kate's life, and I'm sure this stability we fostered contributed to Kate's well-rounded disposition and confidence.

That said, being apart from Kate for weeks at a time wasn't easy, and I'd be remiss if I didn't acknowledge that it affected her as well. I was sad for myself to see her leave, and also sad that we'd ended up in this situation. Still, I was determined to make the best of it. I communicated my feelings openly and made it a point to avoid drama. Our efforts paid off, and the arrangement worked well for Kate. It still meant saying goodbye for a time, but I filled the gap with regular "I'm thinking of you" reminders.

During those years, we didn't yet have cells phones or face-time, but it was essential to stay connected with Kate, while also respecting her time with her Dad. Obviously, I didn't want to interrupt their schedule, their flow, with constant phone calls. But I stayed connected with Kate through handwritten notes I tucked away in her suitcase. I'd prepare notes and cards in advance and marked the envelopes with the dates she could open them. A few envelopes included store-bought cards when the sentiment expressed my feelings perfectly. Sometimes the envelope included homemade cards, stickers, and pictures. On occasion, I'd write a note on a piece of construction paper, cut it up into puzzle pieces, and put them in an envelope—a little challenge to get to the message of the letter. Sometimes I wrote a series of notes, each ending with "to be continued tomorrow." I prepared months in advance, enjoying the creative time and energy behind putting this project together.

These particular notes filled a gap during the extended period we were apart, but we can adapt the same idea to daily life. If you receive an unexpected, thoughtfully designed letter, don't you feel uplifted, even special? This is the way your children feel when they get a random note or surprise from you.

Little everyday notes can be left anywhere. And yes, text messaging makes it easy to send an emoji heart, smiley face, or a quick text. But as I said, those messages can't replace the written word. We hold notes in our hands, and we often save them. They're tangible and long-lasting. The underlying message conveys to your children that you interrupted your day to buy a card, write a note, and then place where it shows up to surprise them.

Leaving these notes around for Kate was a source of sheer pleasure for me, no matter her age. I became more creative about writing the messages and putting them in inconspicuous places. When she was away at college, I mailed cards or simple messages, sometimes as part of a mom care package. I always smiled to myself thinking the notes might deliver an unexpected pick-me-up on a trying day. Serving our children's needs, growth, and security is the responsibility of a servant mother. Never underestimate the power of the written word as a way to express our pride, love, or concern.

NOTES COME FULL CIRCLE

Eventually, this practice of communicating by way of written notes came full circle. When Kate was around age eleven, I interviewed for several new spa director positions, some of which were out of state. I knew that accepting a new job would involve a significant move for Kate and me. One particular opportunity was at the top of my list and after prospecting and interviewing briefly on the phone, we scheduled an in-person interview. I packed my bag, had my family-of-choice relative stay with Kate and headed off for the two-day interview process.

As I unpacked in my room at the resort, inside my suitcase I spotted an envelope. A note from Kate. It was my turn to smile. That evening I opened my prayer book and another little note in the shape of a cutout heart fell to the ground. Her sweetness melted my heart. She duplicated what she'd felt from the messages she'd received over the years. Now I was the lucky recipient. Still young, Kate "got it" and embraced the beauty of the message, "I'm thinking of you."

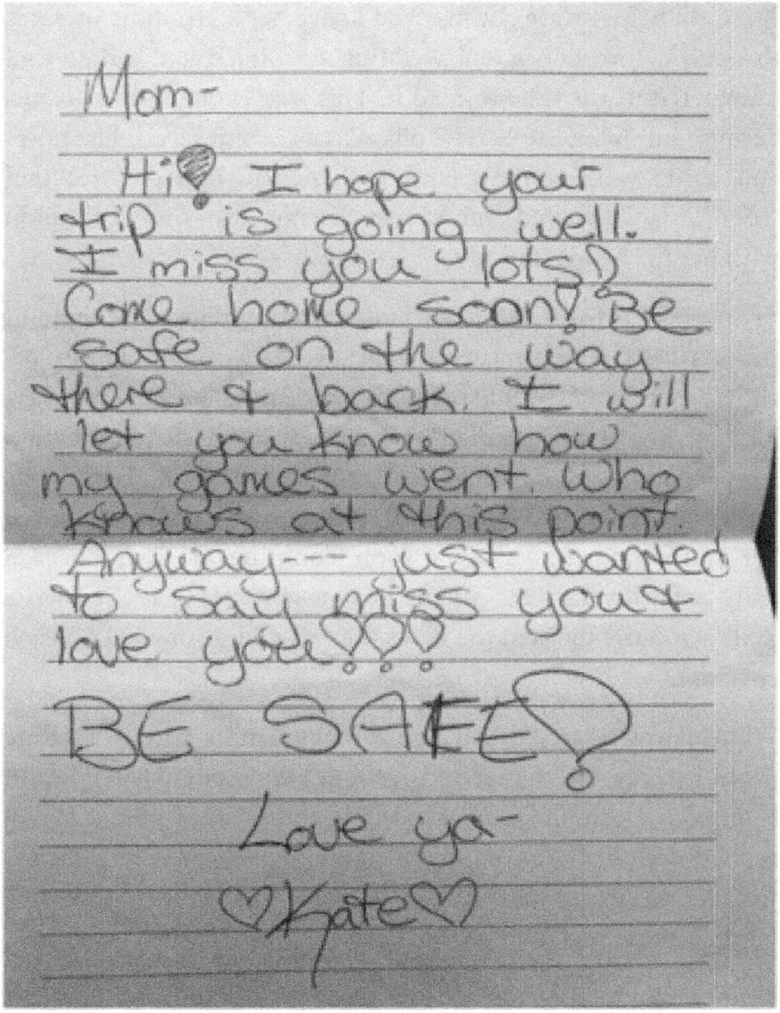

Mom-

Hi! I hope your trip is going well. I miss you lots!) Come home soon! Be safe on the way there & back. I will let you know how my games went. Who knows at this point. Anyway--- just wanted to say miss you & love you!!!

BE SAFE!

Love ya-

Kate

Years later, after Kate married, she sent this "thinking of you" sentiment to a long-time childhood friend struggling with a leukemia diagnosis. Laura had to remain quarantined in the hospital for her bone marrow transplant, so Kate created a box of "notes" and goodies for Laura to open on designated days during her stay. This wasn't the first time she'd done something like that, but I was able to see the gesture firsthand.

A month before Kate got married I gave her a grouping of cards to open before her actual wedding day. Each had a date that designated it was time to read it. This was a tough time for me, because I moving into a new phase as a servant mom. The notes and cards were reminiscent of all her loving qualities that would now be shared and further developed in this new union with her husband Anthony.

As a spa director, I attended industry conferences a couple of times a year, which meant that Aunt B, one of my family-of-choice members, would stay with Kate in our home. Preparing to leave meant organizing the house, fixing meals for the days I'd be gone, and creating notes to leave behind. For weeks before my departure, I'd look for items to let her know I loved her and would return home soon, counting the days on each daily note. Just as I did when she was gone for extended visits with her dad, I marked the dates they should be opened on each envelope.

While I was gone, I'd call home each evening to talk to Kate about her day. On the second evening of my four-day trip, Aunt B answered the phone. I asked how things were going, and B replied with her usual exuberance and light-heartedness. "All is well. Kate is great, the cats are alive and the house is still standing. But there was one tiny hiccup."

My heart jumped.

"Kate was upset last evening."

"What happened?" I was eager to know.

"Kate opened up her card for the evening and we read it together. We got to the end and it was signed, 'Love, Marie' instead of 'Love, Mom'."

Tearful, Kate said, "Mom forgot me already."

Seriously? Kate got on the phone and I apologized for having been distracted, although I couldn't remember how I'd done such an odd thing, other than not being focused while I wrote the cards. In a light-hearted tone, I told her that even moms make mistakes. Kate and I laughed about this incident later. I made a note to myself to pay attention to detail.

YOU HAVE PLENTY TO SAY

To this very day, I send "just because" notes to Kate. Yes, our children grow up but they're never too old to receive a reminder that they are loved and are in our thoughts. This gesture also expresses gratitude, particularly our gratitude for them. A large body of research confirms that grateful people are happier, more hopeful, and healthier. And of course, you're modeling a great way to show appreciation for others through acts of kindness that your child may duplicate one day. We also can't assume our children know how much they are loved, so use opportunities to communicate that in various ways, including with the written word.

Notes can be a vehicle by which you share your pride, and when appropriate, your humility. Sure, a graduation party can be great fun, but a personal note of pride—or awe over the achievement—is held close to the heart forever.

Handwritten notes are also an effective way to offer an apology. Maybe you missed a game you planned to attend, or you had to break a promise. Maybe you want to acknowledge difficult, even contentious times. Maybe you want to express regret for not expressing your love often enough.

Written notes go beyond the power of everyday communication. The same is true for the messages you mail to a child in college or away in the military or taking a first job away from home. A note before a child's wedding will always be a special keepsake.

As our kids grow up right in front of our eyes, they're always on our minds, but seldom do we reflect all that we feel back to them. A note is way to highlight appreciation for the generosity and thoughtfulness you see them express as they mature, perhaps toward their grandparents or special friends. Whatever it is, put it in writing for your children, regardless of their age.

The irony of all of this is that your child may one day become the "note ghost." When your child, young or old, writes you a note or sends a card, you'll cherish the message and save the card... forever.

MOM MEMO
Thinking of You

- Cell phones and texts can't ever replace the special quality of a handwritten note
- Children cherish written messages from parents and may tuck them away as a keepsake, just as you probably do with special letters and cards.
- Taking the time to write notes to our kids sends the message that we're thinking of them—that sticks.
- If you have a difficult time expressing yourself, a greeting card will do—this is why they're still popular and often come in handy.
- Put a stamp on the card or note and mail it. An unexpected, uplifting piece of mail is a bonus these days, and can make a young child feel very special—not so young kids, too.
- A note can be a gentle, thoughtful way to offer an apology or send a special appreciation or congratulations message.

- A card or note, even a sticky note on a mirror, is a tangible—and magical—expression of love and something to hold on to for years.
- Sharing some form of written gratitude with your children for what they have become to family, friends, and others is a gift that keeps on giving.

Mankind's greatest achievements are found on thank you notes, not resumes.

—Wes Fesler, Athlete and Football Coach

TWENTY

Life's Adventures

The measure of who we are is what we do with what we have.

—Vince Lombardi, Football Coach

Parents often are called upon to make major decisions that affect the entire family. We start with the intention of making the right decision for all involved. Let's say we're offered a promotion or a new job, and everything about it, from a salary increase to better benefits, add up to a great opportunity for us and our family—at least it looks good on paper. On the other hand, perhaps our children have special talents or medical needs that would be better served in a new city or state. Financial considerations often come into play as we anticipate future expenses, like college costs or an impending wedding, or we simply want to improve the family's financial situation to stay ahead of rising costs. In other words, we can cite all kinds of reasons that saying yes to a move is advantageous.

Relocating can be both daunting and exciting. I know this is true because as a single mom I had to consider all the changes and adjustments relocation would encompass from school systems and other educational opportunities, to church communities, to affordable housing and neighborhoods. Of course, every move meant both Kate and I were challenged to start over again, so to speak. One move stands out, and having relocated several times before, it wasn't our first rodeo.

At the time, the mid-1990s, the destination Spa and Wellness industry was booming and recruiters searched for potential candidates to fill numerous positions in spas throughout the country. At the time, I was the Director of Spa Operations for Boyne USA, operating out of Northern Michigan and Big Sky, Montana. By the time Kate was twelve, we had already moved relocated once after my divorce, motivated by my longing to be back east, and twice for job opportunities. In each case, I was committed to providing Kate with a solid, steady homelife, as well as a community that would nurture and contribute to her overall wellbeing. I believed then and now that we only reap the benefits we sow. In other words, I couldn't sit back and wait for opportunities to find me. I had to find them myself.

As for Kate, I saw her as a wise child, outgoing and articulate, qualities I prayed would serve her well in new situations. Fortunately, Kate did well in school and loved sports, music and other arts and had a thirst to try new things. I needed to ensure she would continue to develop these qualities and skills during what we all know are the formative years.

I also considered how close we'd be to family. At times we were too far to routinely drive to see relatives, so I had to remedy that situation by assessing the availability of flights. No matter where we went, I was confident we'd connect to a cluster of individuals who would help us create a family of choice, which has been a consistent and important theme in my parenting life. In another chapter, I discussed hospitality and the pleasure Kate and I found in opening our home to others and establishing meaningful relationships. Looking back, I can see that our approach to creating a family of choice reinforced the true meaning of a faith-filled life of hospitality.

Although several job offers came my way, I had to say no if the dynamics surrounding the move didn't work. Maybe it was the school district, or too much distance between my work site and Kate's school. In other cases, the job would require too much travel. When interviewing, I never shied away from saying that my daughter was my priority and my first role was Mom. I have to laugh now thinking how I must have sounded from the other side of the table.

You may be faced with these same dilemmas. I was fortunate to be offered very good opportunities. However, I'm aware that parents, especially single parents who need to find better paying jobs, might be tempted to downplay their priorities as parents in order to secure the position. I didn't do that, and I don't recommend that anyone else do so either, no matter how desperate their situation might seem in the moment. Compromising your most important role in life isn't worth it. I said no to an otherwise good offer in Manhattan and another in Florida because the other priorities, such as schools, affordable housing, and so on, didn't add up.

In retrospect the positions I accepted panned out to be the best one at that time, because all the puzzle pieces fit. Remind yourself, too, that you aren't alone in making these decisions and that you have God at your side. I prayed and listened within to help me decide to accept or decline an offer. I also leaned on other support systems in my life, so my decisions weren't made in a bubble.

A HAPPY ADVENTURE

One of the relocation adventures brought us to Petoskey, Michigan, a town in a region of Northern Michigan often referred to as the "Pine Tree Caribbean." Surrounded by captivating views of Lake Michigan and Little Traverse Bay, this beautiful area is a haven for ski lovers and outdoor enthusiasts. Accepting a new job as Spa Director for a resort company was simultaneously exciting and scary. Things lined up, though, and our house sold quickly, and after the movers drove off, Kate and the two cats and I made the drive up north to our new beginnings.

This advancement in my career gave me an opportunity to invest in Kate's future, and mine. Kate was in middle-school by then, and the local system offered excellent and challenging academic opportunities. Kate adjusted well, even better than what I'd hoped for. (I realize that in families with two or more kids, adjustments may take place on different timetables, so it can take a while for life to settle down.)

We hadn't been in Petoskey for long when I took Kate to a local production of "Charlie and the Chocolate Factory." I was impressed—the kids were outstanding. After the show, Kate said, "I'm going to be in the play next year." She meant it too. When audition time came around the following year, Kate tried out with other students from the surrounding schools and landed the lead in a production of "Charlotte's Web." No kidding. She had practice five days a week and six performances. In addition to memorizing the script, she had to learn musical solos and dance routines. Kate soared as Charlotte, but even more significant were the priceless opportunities to experience commitment, team work, stage presence, and the satisfaction of creative expression.

Many things happened that reinforced the wisdom of my decision to move to Michigan, including Kate's involvement in music and playing flute in the band, being admitted to gifted programs, church commitments, and finally, the development of the trademark program I created, ROUTEEN. I'd found a home in the historic Gaslight District, and we lived only blocks from the Bay. In addition, some key family members in Ohio were a doable six-hour drive away. True, the winter weather was on the brutal side, long, snowy, and cold. Gray skies were typical during the winter months, which created lake effect snow more days than not. The sun was hidden for days on end, and wasn't long before I realized I was affected by seasonal affective disorder (SAD), so I prayed for help with that.

WHEN IT'S TIME TO MOVE ON

Three years passed quickly, and my situation at work began to change. Business was a bit off, and rumors spread about possible closings and staff furloughs and other cost cutting measures. The proverbial handwriting was on the wall, and I stayed tuned in to these changes. When a recruiter called me about an opportunity at a premiere resort in West Virginia, I sent a resume and soon had my first interview. In a matter of weeks, I was invited onsite for the next round. Two days later, I was offered the job of Executive Director of Spa for the well-known Greenbrier Resort. I was speechless. A great career move for sure, plus I could provide well for Kate. It was a career game changer.

Of course, I had to consider that a new job meant another move for Kate. From what I've said, it's clear she was thriving, but my job was in no way secure. Kate was smart and growing in every area. College was only a few years away. All in all, the advantages of the move outweighed the downside. Optimism became my focus as I prepared to highlight to Kate the benefits of this move. I knew this would be a challenging conversation because eighth grade is potentially a tough time to make this kind of transition.

Before accepting Greenbrier's offer, I said I needed to come back for a visit with Kate. I'd pretty much made up my mind about the move, but I wanted more time to check out the area and the school systems, while also having Kate be a part of the decision-making process. Still optimistic, we flew to West Virginia and took a tour around the area and visited the school she'd attend, and even checked out some houses. Then we stopped for lunch, at which point, I saw tears in Kate's eyes. She looked so sad when she said, "This doesn't feel like home."

Ouch. That hurt, but I had a good idea how she felt. She expressed reservations and sadness about starting in a new place...once again. I listened empathetically, because I'd had to move to a different state during my junior year of high school. Like Kate, before the move I'd been happy and doing well in school. I'd created a space for myself where I could do well. No one ever said empathy is always easy, and my heart was heavy and the guilt oppressive, despite knowing this was the right decision given my uncertain work situation. I accepted my uneasiness about Kate's feelings, but stayed silent and let her sit with the situation rather than barging in to attempt to talk her out of her feelings in the service of "making it all better."

ADJUSTING TO BIG CHANGE

The key to getting through this situation was to love Kate through the process. Allowing her to be aware of her feelings created the potential for her to be resilient and brave in her own skin. I provided security and support, which meant being fully present as I walked her through the adjustment to a new school and new surroundings. I committed to attending all her games, concerts, and whatever else came up. The new job required me to schedule occasional short trips, but other than fulfilling that obligation, I'd be in the audience or in the bleachers.

Ultimately, Kate embraced the change and jumped in with both feet. Her outgoing nature allowed her to engage in sports, music, and church activities almost immediately. Prior to the start of the school year, a "village of moms" gathered a group of their daughters to meet Kate. That was a thoughtful gesture and a fabulous way to knock out the dreaded first day of school and the anxiety about standing out as the new kid on the block. This village of moms also connected like-minded teens to kindle the embers of a new friendship. It couldn't have worked out more perfectly, especially because these friendships turned into a roaring fire. After four years of high school together, many of these young women remain friends today.

The move to West Virginia shows the truth of the statement: "God has a plan that's not always for us to know." As it happened, another new relationship blossomed there when Kate met her husband while they both worked at The Greenbrier.

I'd be less than honest if I didn't admit that so many times I wanted to jump in and make things as easy as possible for Kate. However, after the foundational pieces were in place for her, I had to get out of the way and let her handle her entry into freshman year. No walking her through the doors on the first day or calling to check in. I prayed for her strength and protection and let go, confident the person she was would now get her through. The details about outcome weren't up to me.

PARENTING STYLES

There are quite a few made-up monikers for parenting styles, from bulldozer parent, snowplow parent, helicopter parent, and so on. Helicopter parenting is the one we hear most often. It means hovering like a helicopter and then swooping in to fix everything. Unfortunately, that sets kids up for hardship over the long haul. From what I've observed, too much "over-parenting" leads to a lack of self-confidence because children get the message that we don't believe they're capable of handling a problem or getting past a disappointment or loss on their own. As a result, children can become anxious about coping or making a decision, as if they're waiting for someone to rescue them. As I've said before, we must let our kids figure out solutions to their dilemmas. Listen, support, guide, but hovering and swooping do more harm than good.

A CONCEPT, NOT A LABEL

The parenting concept that's positive and resonates with me is the "Lighthouse parent," perhaps because it evokes lakes or oceans and my favorite places, shorelines and beaches. But it's also descriptive of our potential to be a beacon of light for our children. We can shine so they can see you remaining strong and reliable while they ride the waves of life. There are storms and the risk of hitting some rocks along the way. We all get banged up now and then, but at times, parents can help kids avoid the rocks while still body surfing.

Kenneth Ginsburg, MD, a pediatrician and author of many books about raising resilient, thriving children, created the Lighthouse parent concept and defined it as a "stable force." Lighthouses remain strong and steadfast regardless of what's happening around them. They can be seen in the distance and expose potential hazards, and as parents we can prepare our children to face the rocks and ride the waves. In short, preparation is protection.

This Lighthouse parenting approach resonated with me, at least in part because of the images associated with it. The massive power of the sea, the life below the surface, the sound of the waves, the smell of the salt air, and the warmth of the sand between my toes speak to my soul. Sunrise or sunset, this is where I spend time with God. The lighthouse, a tower of power, speaks to servant leadership, servant motherhood, and the practice of remaining a constant force for those out in the middle of the ocean. As servant moms we're present as our kids navigate the sea of life, and we will stay conscious that our light will shine as both a guide and a ray of hope when our kids are challenged by inevitable storms.

At Sunday mass a few years ago, lighthouses were theme of our pastor's homily. Father Dan cited Biblical references to the call to "let your light shine" and "Nor do they light a lamp and put it under a bushel" (Matthew 5:16), and finally "Let light shine out of darkness, (2 Corinthians 4:6). The pastor asked us to consider another symbol of being the light of the world, the lighthouse. Lighthouses are stoic structures and reliable beacons of light, which represent the love of God shining outward for all to see, not turned inward and hidden. Father Dan's challenge was that we be lighthouses shining our light, faith, hope, and love outward.

As our light shines through the darkness and the fog, we become a glimmer of hope for those struggling. In other words, filled with God's love, we can be a source of light for others. Not an easy task, but our love and security are the guides, the stable force, the lighthouse, for anyone reaching for the light. As a servant mom, a servant parent, we have opportunities to be beacons of light to guide our children safely to shore.

Life throws lots of curveballs and unexpected forks in the road on our journeys, but it's also an adventure and our attitude determines the success or failure of our experiences. For example, if Kate had observed me being really anxious and nervous over our move to West Virginia, and fretting over the changes in her life, my emotions would have spilled over to her. If you find yourself facing a time of upheaval in your life, avoid turning it into a fearful, chaotic time, no matter how difficult it is to navigate. If you manage your stress and anxiety, your children will more easily follow your lead. If you're calm, they will be, too, or at least they'll be less nervous about the changes they face. Even better, if you're enthusiastic about the coming change, sooner or later, they'll catch that spirit of adventure.

Although no parent is perfect, we model either optimism or pessimism. Which is it going to be? A half empty glass or one that's half full and waiting to be topped off. Encourage meaningful "what if" questions with answers focused on the best outcomes, not the worst. On the other hand, you can also be a silent guide for your children's struggle with change, remembering that not every child in the family will react in exactly the same way to change and uncertainty. You are the barometer in the event of change—and the lighthouse beacon guiding the way.

MOM MEMO
Life's Adventures

- Job changes and relocations are two common, often unavoidable life changes, but they can be both fun adventures and difficult adjustments. Be confident and know that you can fulfill your job as a decision maker and simultaneously help your kids through times of painful change,

- Some decisions will be a new adventure for one or more children but may be a major loss for another, so put a plan in place to ease that child's adjustments.
- Resist the urge to fix every problem in your child's life. As heart wrenching as it is to watch sometimes, helicopter parenting has negative consequences.
- Become a Lighthouse parent, a beacon of light, a stable force. Listen and offer ideas and guidance, knowing your support is critical, but you can't adjust or cope for your kids.
- As much as possible, encourage your children to embrace the adventure inherent in changes of all kinds.

Stand strong and discover who you are before someone tells you what you are supposed to be.

—Marie Mozzi

Afterword

By now I hope you're inspired and are empowered to experience the true joy servant motherhood brings. Accepting the work required to be successful involves exploring the "self" you are today while discovering how that "self" came to be. I encourage you to take the journey. Cheerfully embrace whatever inner unrest and apprehension you encounter as you confront your childhood scripts, along with the emotions, stories, and questions embedded in your own history that are still shaping your life today.

As you've seen from my journey as a mom, I've dealt with my share of "coulda done that," or "shoulda known," or "I woulda done this or that differently" scenarios. Yet by taking on the work of unraveling the past, I managed to avoid the turmoil of the terrible twos and turbulent teenage years, too often filled with arguments and conflicts. Even with all the challenges we faced, including being a single parent and making it through some inevitable childhood hiccups, my confident, compassionate and strong child matured into a fine young woman. That's what I want for you as a parent. My hope is that you will look back on the years spent raising your children with the sense that you'd do it all over again with an open heart.

It would be ignorant to think that anyone comes through childhood unscathed, but I do know this: *It's possible to create a home without toxic garbage from the past creeping in and without negative attitudes and power plays creating conflict.* Think of you and your children as embarking on an uncharted voyage together, and along the way you laugh, giggle, and cry, even as you remain a parent and not a friend.

Resolving the conflicts and challenges presented in almost every chapter in this book came down to communication in one form or another, and effective communication takes time and practice. To keep your bond with your children close, even in troubled times, it's key to devote uninterrupted time to be present with your child and truly listen. I recommend dedicating time for breaks from your routine, that include special getaway days for all your children, or whenever possible, one-on-one events with each child. Take vacations if you can, with visits that include chosen family and friends. For many of us, a family of choice enriches our day-to-day lives in countless ways. These families of the heart also provide opportunities to give and receive affection while showing our children what healthy relationships look like.

As you probably know by now, when you make faith a priority in your home, you're able to apologize when you need to and release the notion that you must always be right. By embracing the reality of potential conflict and being willing to engage in difficult conversations, I empowered my daughter to be aware of her voice in every situation, and to know she had the right to be heard. On my part, there was no yelling or screaming, or dramatic overreacting to the proverbial spilled milk.

I've told you my story of pursuing professional help in order to constructively work to uncover my codependency issues that had led me to believe it was my job to make everyone happy—as though somehow, it was even in my power to do so. Eventually, in a healthier and realistic way, I learned to dance with intimacy with myself, my daughter, and others. You can do that, too. If you feel the need for professional help, find it. If insurance coverage is an issue, explore community clinics and counseling services that offer fees based on your ability to pay, or ask a social worker or your minister or other clergy to help you find what you need. Help is available.

At times, every mother, indeed every parent, walks with the fear of failing. However, when these feelings taunted me, I was able to put what I'd learned in counseling to work by embracing and confronting my fears. This is what I wanted for my daughter, and I prayed that I could model this approach for her so that she could see how to confront her own challenges, and you can do the same thing.

A profound piece of this parenting journey was learning the art of being present, to being available to my daughter in more than just the physical sense. This is one of the most important jobs of parenting, but depending on circumstances, it can be one of the toughest. Distractions and a wandering mind are characteristic of modern life and developed well before email, cell phones, and texting intruded even more. In today's world, being present and listening may be one of your biggest challenges.

I worked hard to show up in person for Kate's activities, cheering courtside at her games, and clapping in the audience as she finished a performance. As you may know from your own experience, moms and dads often work late, go to work early, take on extra hours or days at the workplace, and so forth, simply so they can be physically present and be their kids' number one fan. I had to do a lot of time juggling to make that possible.

Valuable as your physical presence is, it's just as important to be emotionally present. This issue goes beyond the tendency to think we can multitask and listen with one ear while doing half a dozen other things. It also means you unpack your own concerns at that moment, especially emotional garbage, and get it out of the way.

We tend to project and misalign our own thoughts and actions on someone else if we don't deal with them first. That's what I explained when we started this journey, and why getting the help I needed made all the difference to becoming the kind of servant mom I strived to be. Your "junk" will get in the way of being present and listening. Your history, past relationships, repressed anger and other emotions have a way of rearing their ugly heads. Unwittingly, our children can be the recipients of this unaddressed garbage. That said, yes, you and your parenting are always a work in progress, so don't add another burden by expecting perfection. Always strive to simply be a better version of yourself

The notion of a family of choice has come up often in these chapters, and that's because it's a real thing. My heart is filled with gratitude for the people that have helped form and mold a great piece of who Kate is today. They have been the definition of hospitality, welcoming us when we were strangers, and becoming our village. We moved more than I'd ever imagined, but the new villages we encountered were filled with people who became family to us. Kate learned that she and I could extend the same welcome to others. We maintain contact with members of our chosen families and always will through cards, calls, virtual hellos, or in-person visits. You may be a person who welcomes others and models that for your children, or perhaps you're the family that's on the move. Either way, you will enrich your family's life by including others into your ever-expanding social circle.

Some of you may also be single parents, like I was, or perhaps your children have a step parent or have added siblings through remarriage. Although I didn't delve deeply into this topic, I maintained a healthy relationship with Kate's dad so she could enjoy knowing her paternal grandparents and her many cousins. Our arrangement worked because I was always accepted as Kate's mom, and I valued my former husband's relatives as Kate's forever family. We've maintained strong bonds to this day.

So, if you find yourself in contentious situations with a former spouse or your in-law family, or your own family behaves in an unhealthy way toward your children's in-law family members, then do whatever it takes to fix it. Children pick up on tensions and resentments and that can poison family life and lead to petty gossip or even open hostility. These are common issues in therapy and in family and spiritual counseling. Don't let these unpleasant situations fester because they seldom get better on their own.

Bottom line, I didn't become a mother by myself and do the whole job alone—and that's how it should be. I'm grateful for all the help, support, and love that entered the picture in a variety of venues. You aren't alone, either, even if it can sometimes feel that way. I don't know your situation and what obstacles you faced when you became a mandatory mom and committed to being a servant mother, but if you find yourself troubled and facing challenges that could overwhelm you or anyone, then first turn to your faith and faith community to seek the help and support you need.

Along with the heavy dose of gratitude, I'm proud of both my daughter and myself. Digging deep and confronting questions and fears helped me become a better servant mom: present, fair, motivating, and fun-loving. The inner work also enabled me to set boundaries, and stick to my guns about respect, trust and communication.

My trust in God allowed me to rely on my faith even in the toughest of moments and was my foundation for embracing this role of a servant mom. Fighting through the feelings of unworthiness, fear of being a failure, or feelings of inadequacy could have plagued my mind and spirit. They entered often enough but I knew that I had to keep turning to God to help me through, no matter what state I was in. I prayed for guidance and support when I was tired, overwhelmed, or temporarily struck with fear.

I heard a fabulous quote that stuck with me years ago. "God doesn't call the equipped, He equips the called." When we're confident, it's easy to show up to do the right things. But it takes faith and trust in God's will for us when we must take a risk and dive into troubled or confusing waters. But it's during those times that God's plan is revealed to us. Many times I sat alone in tears, asking God why certain situations appeared in my life, or I wanted to know the reason for a particular disappointment. I knew God had a plan. God's ways are not our ways, nor are His thoughts ours. I'd be lying if I denied occasionally wishing I'd known the plan. Most of us can plead guilty to wanting clarity and certainty, even when we know that's not how faith works. However, I remained steadfast, and now, years later, I see it all. How foolish I was to question the plan.

The truth of God's love is that He has a plan for us. Staying vigilant and trusting when tough times present themselves is the journey of the faithful. Have faith, stay the course, and lean into God. Pray for mercy and grace, celebrating every win and every challenge. If you begin to question whether you are doing a good enough job, remember God is providing you with the tools for servant motherhood. I know my prayers were answered, keeping me centered and focused on my vocation as a mom. My heart was wrapped around this responsibility of nurturing and caring for this gift He sent, my beautiful daughter.

So, embrace your servant mom role. Whether you have one, two, or ten kids, you are a part of their destiny, their journey. No one has a greater impact on a child than a parent. (No pressure, huh?) The importance of your influence is also why being kind and loving to yourself, and making time to care for your needs is critical. When your children see your self-care, they carry that attribute into their future role as parents.

Your confidence and skill as a servant mom is a great nurturing model for your sons, but it has even more significance for your daughters, because someday they might envision being a servant mom themselves, and because of you, they will be well prepared.

"Well done my good and faithful servant."
—Matthew 25:21

Additional Resources

Throughout this book, I mentioned books that offered insights and greatly enriched my journey. Now, I'm encouraging you to collect these and other resources as you explore ways to grow and deepen your life as a servant mother.

Birth, A Guide for Prayer. Bergan & Schwan. Revised 2020, Saint Mary's Press, and *Love: A Guide for Prayer.* 2011. Loyola Press.

Daring Greatly, Brown, Brené. 2012. Gotham Books, and *Dare to Lead.* 2018. Random House Publishing Group.

Intentional Living. Maxwell, John. 2015. Hatchette Book Group, and *The 21 Irrefutable Laws of Leadership.* 2007. Thomas Nelson, Inc.

Purpose Driven Life. Warren, Pastor Rick. 2002. Zondervan Books.

The Seven Levels of Intimacy: The Art of Loving and the Joy of Being Loved. Matthew Kelly, 2005. Beacon Publishing.

The 5 Love Languages. Chapman, Gary. 2014. Northfield Publishing.

Codependent No More: How to Stop Controlling Others and Start Caring for Yourself. Beattie, Melodie. 1986, Second edition. Hazelden Publishing

Toxic Parents. Forward, Susan. 1989. Bantam Books.

The Dance of Intimacy: A Woman's Guide to Courageous Acts of Change in Key Relationships. Lerner, Harriet. 2009. Harper-Collins e-books.

Body, Mind, Sport. Douillard, John. 2001, Revised Edition. Three Rivers Press.

About the Author

Marie is an unstoppable force who infuses positive change in those around her. *Witnessing the empowerment and success of others is what truly lights her fire!* Encouraging individuals to untether their limiting beliefs from scripts of the past in favor of finding new ways of living in the present.

She has been a corporate executive director, teacher and coach as well as a competitive athlete and fitness professional. Informed by a servant leadership philosophy Marie is a speaker, trainer, youth minister and Spiritual Director. As a woman of faith, she knows that her ability to lead and display heartfelt concern for others isn't something she's doing alone. God is in the driver's seat. For more information, visit www.-mariemozzi.com.

Made in the USA
Monee, IL
09 June 2025

19106204R00164